John & Anne,

Thanks for being
part of my life!

Stan

Take This Job and Love It

All It Takes Is All Ya Got

by Stan Reeg

with Rich Wolfe

Photo Credits: Stan Reeg
Layout: The Printed Page, Phoenix, AZ
Author's agent: T. Roy Gaul
Cover Poster Design/Copy: Rich Wolfe

Rich Wolfe can be reached by email at rjwolfe52@gmail.com or by cell phone at 602-738-5889

ISBN: 978-0-692-03557-3

CONTENTS

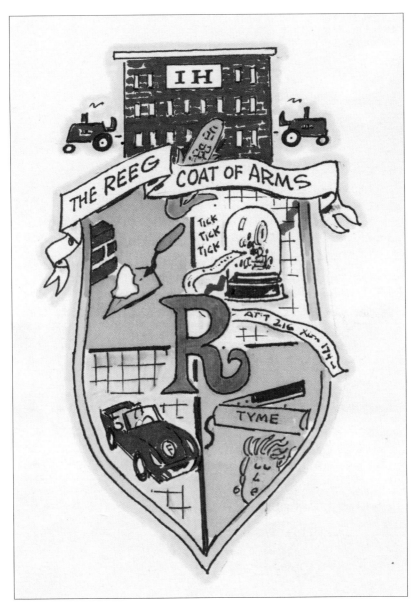

New Reeg Coat of Arms designed by author for this book.

PREFACE

"St. Donatus, Iowa? You're from St. Donatus, Iowa?"

I couldn't believe it. It was in a beautiful hospitality tent at a PGA golf tournament when I was introduced to Stanley Reeg. When he said he was from this tiny Iowa town, forty miles from where I grew up, I found it hard to believe. Nobody comes from that small town. The town has 132 people, about evenly divided between men and women.

St. Donatus is a beautiful town, certainly not what you would expect in Iowa, more like you would see in the Netherlands or Luxembourg.

Talking with Stan, it became more incredulous—his history of working in a factory for many years, the factory closing, he goes to a community college for career advice. They advise him to become a stockbroker, which made no sense at all. He becomes a stockbroker, and he does exactly what they tell him to do in training class. No one does what they tell them to do in training class in that business. The trainers demand that a newcomer contact 25 people a day with cold calls and actually talk to them. It's not like dialing 25 numbers and hanging up or getting a voicemail. You have to actually talk to a decision-maker and do that five days a week, fifty-two weeks a year and keep a record of it. Well, Stanley Reeg did that, and guess what? He became enormously successful, loved by his clients, and a multi-millionaire.

Every winter for five months, I host a monthly luncheon at Orange Tree Golf Club in Scottsdale, Arizona. It consists of mostly retired business leaders from Iowa that have winter homes in Arizona. Stan was invited to join, and it was amazing how well he fit in from Day One. Now he's one of the most popular members of that group.

A question people ask, "Who the heck is going to buy a book like this?" Broker office managers nationwide will buy this book and give it to every newcomer they have. The training schools where brokerage companies train their new recruits will buy them or encourage the trainees to buy them. Entrepreneurs will buy the book. Iowans will buy the book, particularly Iowans with a small-town background.

But I'm not so concerned with selling books. I've sold over two million copies in my career. I'm more interested in having fun, and I picked the right guy. Stanley was fabulous. He did everything asked him. He did it promptly and did it well. It's just been a total joy to do this book. He's a heck of a guy. It's been fun, and here's hoping you really enjoy it.

Signed,

Rich Wolfe

Rich Wolfe
Scottsdale, Arizona

Chapter 1

DRINKING: THE LAST REFUGE OF SCOUNDRELS

One Drink was Too Many Too Much Wasn't Enough

My first memories of growing up in St. Donatus, Iowa all center around a common theme, and that is of struggle. Growing up poor in rural Iowa meant having struggles for some of our most basic needs like food, shelter and clothing. My father was a functioning alcoholic, which did not make things any easier for my Mom, who had her own struggles in raising seven children. Her ability to make the best of not-so-good circumstances influenced each of us in that those struggles gave rise to strong desires to not just get by, but to create results. Through it all, I've always considered myself a very lucky person, and luck had a lot to do with my successes, but hard work was needed every step of the way...this is my story.

Dad worked at John Deere in Dubuque for 30 years, from 1948 to 1978. I was home only until 1964. Most of the time, he worked as a machinist on the day shift, which was 7 a.m. to 3 p.m. In the last 10 of his years there, he worked as a tractor repairman on the small crawlers.

Interestingly enough, when I started at Farmall in 1965, my first job was a tractor repairman as well. Dad's job was on the crawlers, while mine was on the International Harvester Farmall red tractors. Anyway, he drove to work in his car by himself sometimes, and he carpooled with other workers from around St. Donatus other times.

Back in the 1950s and early '60s, John Deere and Dubuque Packing Company provided the best-paying jobs around the area. They provided great benefits for people that didn't have advanced educations, and this was Dad's case. He quit school after the seventh grade and started working as a hired hand on farms.

Many afternoons on the way home from work, Dad and his car crew would stop at a bar or two. Many evenings, it would be midnight when Dad got home from work.

When he got home late, he would holler until one of the boys would get out of bed to fix him something to eat. After I did that a few times in the middle of the night, I decided I'd fix him. The next couple of times he got me out of bed to cook for him, I just started burning whatever food he wanted me to prepare for his midnight snack! After that, he quit hollering for me, and he started hollering for my brothers Billy or Mickey until they would get up to fix him something to eat. I suspect that is the reason I've never taken any interest in cooking and probably will not in the future.

Stan Reeg lived in this Weber stonehouse from 1952 until 1963. No well, no running water, fully equipped with an outhouse 30 feet from the front door.

In 1953, we moved over to an old rock house, which was a mile and a half west of St. Donatus. If Dad came home directly from work and then later in the evening decided to go back to town (St. Donatus or St. Catherine) Mom would send me with him since I was the oldest. She thought that would encourage him to come home earlier. Guess what? That usually didn't work. Many nights when those bars closed down at midnight, he and his drinking buddies would go to East

Dubuque, Illinois, because they served alcohol and the bars were open until 3 a.m.

I can remember many late nights sitting in one of their cars freezing and waiting until they decided it was finally time to go home. I would sometimes wait three hours in below-zero temperatures wondering when in the heck he would be coming out so we could go home. Since I was just a kid, I couldn't go into the bar to persuade him to go home. The next morning, he would have the Brown Bottle Flu.

Then when Dad got home, he always turned down the thermostats on the kerosene oil burners to save money. It was the middle of the winter, and we had those oil burners only on the main floor. It was a two-story house, and we kids all slept upstairs while Mom and Dad had their master bedroom on the main level. As a matter of fact, sometimes in the cold of the winter when it was 20 below zero outside, we would wake up in the morning with white frost on the windows as well as on the inside stone walls—and the walls were 12- to 16-inches thick! Some nights we would take the clothes we were going to wear to school the next day to bed with us so they would be warm in the morning. We used to joke that when it got even colder, they would just throw another brother on the bed.

At the stone house, there was no well, no running water, no indoor plumbing or bathroom, and no other amenities. We would brag that we had furniture that was imported from Dubuque. In fact, we had a dirt floor in the cellar (or basement, as you would call it), and we stored the potatoes that we had grown the previous summer.

The outhouse furnished with a Sears Roebuck catalog which was not used as reading material!

The worst thing about living in that house was going to the outhouse in the middle of the night in the winter. Just think, a foot of snow and temperatures of minus 20. We kept our drinking, cooking, laundry, and bathing water in two five-gallon cream cans. Once I was big enough to drive Dad's car (long before I was 16), he would send me to the landlord's place at the top of the hill to fill those two cans with water and haul them back on the back floor of his car. Sometimes I would take one of my siblings with me, and that was fine because I started driving at a very young age and generally when we were driving, we would be spinning the tires somewhere.

I don't recall ever going to Grandpa and Grandma Adams' farm by Lancaster, Wisconsin, at Christmas. They were Mom's parents and, for some reason, Dad always despised visiting Mom's side of the family. Whenever we were driving to visit any of Mom's relatives in Lancaster, Fennimore, Cassville, or Platteville, Wisconsin (which were only about 50 miles away), Dad had a habit of stopping at Sandy Hook, which was a tavern just across the Wisconsin state line, or at a roadhouse by Tennyson, Wisconsin, which was just a few more miles up the road.

While we were all sitting in the car, he would go in and have drinks, and we never knew if he would have one drink or if we were going to be sitting in the car waiting for him an hour or more. It seemed like he needed a drink to face Mom's family. I still don't understand what his issue was. Mom's family members always treated him like family. There was always plenty of alcohol involved when we visited them. In fact, I remember one Sunday afternoon when we were at Grandpa Adams' farm, and the uncles and in-laws were all sitting around out in the front yard. It was a nice summer day, and Mom's brothers were passing the whiskey bottle around. Nearby, they had a red Ball Mason jar lid, and they decided they would pour some whiskey in it and see if the roosters that were running around the yard would drink it. After the rooster sipped enough whiskey, it was stumbling around just like a drunkard would. Of course, it made great entertainment for all the guys and us kids, as we all laughed like we were crazy.

> "Wisconsin: Come Smell Our Dairy Air"

In the 1950s and early '60s, most of Dad's activities—other than working at John Deere—revolved around drinking and hanging out at bars. We felt that if Dad could live his life over, he would live over a bar.

Two months after I met Betty, I went to her parents' house for Christmas. Christmas was an over-the-top experience, and it was the holiday of the year. Her mother, Kay McCarthy, always baked and made candies, cookies, and meals. She also purchased many gifts for everyone in the family. The previous 12 or 14 years, Christmas was a depressing experience for me. Once I was aware there was no Santa Claus, Dad gave me cash in an envelope instead of a personal gift. Then a week later, when he was broke, he would borrow it back from me. I never saw the money again. He did the same thing to my sister Judy.

On Christmas afternoons, we were always invited over to Grandpa and Grandma Reeg's house for opening gifts and a nice dinner. It was about a five-mile trip from our house up a gravel road through the timber. The road was very steep, and many times we would get stuck in the snow trying to get up to their house. Some of the taverns near our town served free alcohol and drinks to their customers on Christmas morning. With Dad being the drinker he was, he couldn't pass up that opportunity!

Many Christmas afternoons were scary times for us because when Dad came home after drinking all morning, we didn't know if he was going to be jolly, mean, or just drunk. One year when he came home, Mom told him, "I don't know why you think you have to drink like you do!" He really got mad and kicked out the front wood-framed door. That's how he disciplined my brothers as well. He always wore steel-toed shoes when he worked at the John Deere factory, and his favorite method of disciplining us was kicking us in the butt with his foot. Man, did we hate that!

I am not sure why he had to drink like that, because his parents did not drink a lot. Dad had a chip on his shoulder most of his adult life. The only time he seemed to be happy was when he was drinking. Now that I look back on it, I feel bad for him! When we were young children, one of our concerns was that Dad could get seriously injured in a fight. Fortunately, he never did. But then I wonder why none of us kids are alcoholics. Our Mother was filled with faith and was a very positive influence in our lives. Actually, it is a wonder we older boys even drink alcohol after what we experienced in our childhood!

On one of those late nights, Dad and two friends were in St. Donatus drinking for several hours, then they decided to go to East Dubuque. I was the only child with them. Larry Berendes had a brand new '56 Chevy. Dad was sitting in the front seat, while Larry was driving. We were on the East Dubuque Bridge, when Larry sideswiped another car. His car then hit the side of the bridge and rolled over. We skid off of the bridge toward the end of the abutment. The car was on its side, and when it stopped moving, there I was—a little innocent child with a 200-pound man on top of me!

Needless to say, all the Iowa bars were closed, as it was well after midnight. Larry was already intoxicated. He totally demolished the new Chevy. He ended up in jail with a DWI. I didn't get hurt, but my ego and hip were bruised. In 1956, I was 10. It is remarkable that none of us were injured in that accident, as we were not wearing seat belts. Seat belts were an option on the new cars at that time. I can't seem to recall how the three of us got home that night from East Dubuque. It may have been a friend of the East Dubuque Police Department that drove us home.

It was generally worse when Dad did not come home directly from work. We were living in the old stone house, where the window wells were more than a foot deep. Many nights, we would take turns sitting in those windows, looking for hours on end, hoping and praying that Dad would come driving over the hill. We were in a valley. We kept looking up that hill, expecting the next car headlights coming over the hill to be Dad's. Many nights he didn't show up until long after we went to bed. Mom would feed us dinner, and we just went to bed disappointed again.

There were times on Friday afternoons when Dad got paid and he and his buddies left John Deere Tractor Works at 3 p.m. and would stop at a tavern supposedly to cash their checks. Sometimes Dad didn't show up at home until late Saturday afternoon or evening because they were out drinking and carousing all night and into the next afternoon. When I look back on those days, I'm not sure how it emotionally impacted me and my siblings. I guess it was part of the "gristmill of life" and we learned something from it.

The story that really caps off Dad's drinking days is what happened one summer Saturday afternoon in Bellevue. Dad took us to purchase new shoes before going back to school. Earlier in the day, he had been drinking. When he came home to get Mom and all of us kids, he was already intoxicated, or "loaded" as we called it. He ended up in the bars again for hours. Finally toward dusk, we were all heading back home in the four-door 1955 Chevy. Mom never had a driver's license, so Dad was driving. On the way home, still within the Bellevue city limits on River Drive, he drove over about a five-inch curb on to the river embankment and the car was still moving. Below us about 40 feet down was the Mississippi River. He might have been driving only 30 miles an hour, but at that point, I was sitting on the driver's side in the back seat, and my brother Billy was sitting right next to me. I said to Bill, "I'm jumping out of here. I am not drowning in the Mississippi River." I opened the door and bailed out with Billy following immediately behind me. We walked across the street to a house. We knocked on the door and the people kindly invited us in. We told them what had just happened, and they came outside with us to see what was going on.

Mom convinced Dad to turn the car around to find us. We were standing in the yard appearing a little befuddled when Mom saw us standing there and told Dad to turn into the driveway. We got in, and we all went home.

The next thing you know, a week or so later, my Mom and Dad received a letter and a summons for them and all seven of us kids to appear in front of the Jackson County Human Services Department in Maquoketa, Iowa, at a specific date and time. On the appointed day, Mom dressed us all up in our Sunday best, and Dad threatened us, "If you don't practice your best behavior and keep your mouths shut at the hearing, you'll pay for it when we get home!" I don't remember any of the inquisition or hearing, but I do remember later on Grandma Reeg telling me how terrible it would be if "some or all of you kids were to become wards of the state." I am sure she was quite worried about the whole affair, as she was a Nervous Nellie anyway.

It has been a long time since I've thought about many of these experiences. They were all painful events and memories. I thought I blocked most of them out of my memory, but I realize I have not. I would not want to go through many of these experiences again, but I don't regret having gone through them because that is part of what has made me and my siblings what we are today. I will say one thing about Dad, and that is, no matter how much he drank the night before or how late he got home, he always went to work the next morning. He always preached, especially to me and my brothers, "You take care of your job." Fortunately, he worked at many well-paying jobs at Deere for 30 years and was able to retire on a nice pension. He lived 28 years in retirement—almost as long as he worked at Deere—and virtually every year, Deere increased his pension payment.

Because most of the money Dad made at Deere was spent at bars, we never had much for clothes, toys, and food. Many of our clothes were hand-me-downs, and they weren't the warmest in the wintertime. Every day, we would walk a mile-and-a-half each way to and from St. Donatus Catholic Grade School. I remember those cold winter mornings when I, being the oldest, would encourage my siblings to hurry up and walk or run to the top of Weber's Hill. The guy driving the milk truck would not stop in the middle of the hill to pick us up, but if we were on top of the hill, he would stop and haul us over to St. Donatus. Many of the times we just walked the whole distance despite the weather. The rides were always much appreciated, especially on bitter cold winter mornings!

Occasionally, Mr. Neff would give us a ride. The Neffs were an affluent family from Dubuque who had a couple of children.

They owned a summer home that was about a mile east of us, close to the Mississippi River. Whenever we got a ride to school with them, he and the children were praying the rosary as we drove to St. Donatus.

Actually, most of my growing up years until 1964, you would have considered my Dad an alcoholic. Interestingly enough, one Sunday in late 1963, the whole family went a few miles out west of Bellevue to visit Dad's first cousin Harvey Duesing. Harvey and Dad liked to drink, and they proceeded to drink a fifth of whiskey and a case of beer that Sunday. On the drive home, Dad told Mom he was going to quit drinking, and she just laughed at him. He was so strong willed that he could not be tempted to even taste a drink of alcohol the next seven years. He started drinking again sometime in 1971, but at a more moderate pace.

Dad was like Grandma Reeg's brothers Allen and Vincent Ernst, who were very strong willed. During Dad's later drinking days in the late 1950s, one Saturday at 6:30 a.m., we were awakened by someone incessantly blowing a car horn. It was his uncle Vince Ernst, who was on one of his "overnight tooters" as we called it then—now I would call it a drinking binge. He hollered out of the Studebaker car window, "Come on, Bill. Let's go have a few drinks." When Dad was drinking in Bellevue, Andrew or Preston, with Uncle Vincent in those days, they seemed to get into a lot of fistfights with other patrons at the taverns and bars.

We found out that beer is more than a breakfast drink!

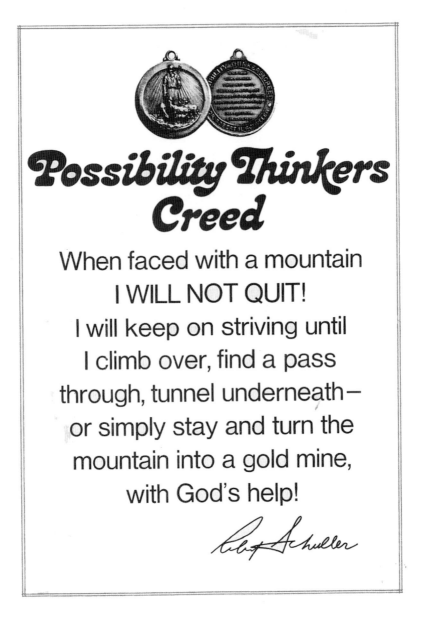

Possibility Thinkers Creed

When faced with a mountain
I WILL NOT QUIT!
I will keep on striving until
I climb over, find a pass
through, tunnel underneath—
or simply stay and turn the
mountain into a gold mine,
with God's help!

Robert Schuller

Chapter 2

WHEN WE WERE YOUNG AND OUR WORLD WAS NEW

Stan Reeg celebrating his third birthday.

12-Years-Old Forever

St. Donatus Catholic Grade School

My early schooling was in a four-story stone structure that was built as St. Mary's Academy and Boarding School in 1869 at St. Donatus, Iowa. St. Donatus is a town of 132 people in eastern Iowa near the Mississippi River. The nearest big town is Dubuque, Iowa. By the time I started attending classes there, the second floor was divided into two classrooms where all eight grades of classes were taught.

I started the first grade in 1952, at age six. I was the only student in my class, and after the first year, the principal called my parents and said she believed I was bright enough to take all my second grade classes and third grade English and math classes the next year. She said that after successfully completing those classes, I would be promoted to the fourth grade, where there would then be three of us: Richard Mesch who lived in downtown St. Donatus, Bobby Weber, a farm boy, and myself.

When I was in second grade, I fell off the school playground swing and broke my right forearm. At that time, we were still living in a house where we walked a mile to school with neighboring kids. A couple of the older boys were Donny and Larry Thoma, the two "Big Bullies." They enjoyed picking on us because we wore hand-me-down clothes and were the poorest-dressed kids in school. Shortly after I broke my arm, my brother Billy was riding on a circular trapeze-type device that went around like a merry-go-round. You hung on to a handle by a chain that hung down from the metal canopy. The Thoma bullies would grab one of the handles and run in a circle as fast as they could. One day, Billy was trying to hang on when the Thoma boys were spinning it as fast as possible. Billy lost his grip, fell, and broke his leg.

When I was in fourth grade, the principal, Sister Seraphica, who always thought I was a good little boy, had a revelation. With the facility being so old, there were always things that needed to be repaired. Somehow, the nuns selected me and Bobby Weber's older brother Eldon to be handymen. During the afternoon school hours, Eldon and I were always doing repairs and talking about what we were going to do when we grew up. After Eldon graduated from grade school, he went out into the work world. He started a masonry construction company where he poured many of the cement basements for new homes in Eastern Iowa, Illinois, and Wisconsin. Later, he started another very successful construction company in Indiana and became a millionaire. Unfortunately, he developed cardiac problems when he was young and died when he was 60.

The classrooms were all on the second floor. On the ground floor, there was an artistically decorated quaint chapel where we were encouraged to attend daily Mass. With Mom being very religious, she pushed us to attend. The nuns all lived on the ground floor.

During the seven years I attended St. Donatus Catholic Grade School, the Sisters of Notre Dame from Mankato, Minnesota, were in charge. They graded us as: "Fail," "Fair," "Good," "Very Good," or "Excellent." Overall, I was a pretty good student and ended up with mostly "Very Good" and "Excellent" marks. Most of the time while I was in school, especially from 1953 through 1963, we lived in an old rock house a mile and a half west of St. Donatus. We lived on an acre plot where there were a few other buildings in addition to the house. The property was surrounded by tillable bottom acreage, timber, pastures, and a creek. We older boys were always running around exploring and playing games like Cowboys and Indians that we observed on TV. The summers flew by very fast, as we were kept quite busy. Dad always planted a large garden, and we older boys were expected to hoe the rows and keep the weeds out of it.

When we got bored or couldn't entertain ourselves, Mom would come up with activities for us. Since there were seven of us kids, she would organize a game of softball for us, and she was always the pitcher. She made us choose teams, and she didn't go for the idea that just because I was the oldest that I should get first pick all the time. Even in those early days, I was motivated to win! Each day, we had two team captains who picked their teammates for that day. If it was too hot, she would have us come in the house to play checkers, Yahtzee, cards, and other games. Those were the times that created the great family bond all of us siblings have developed. In many families today, the siblings are estranged or don't get along with each other. That seems like a foreign idea to me, as we are all best friends in our family.

> "Mom was playing both ends against the middle: the accordion."

Mom said that "birds of a feather flock together" and always warned us to be selective about with whom we spent our time. Perhaps the reason I don't have more close friends is that I am independent. I know I can count on myself, but I'm not sure I can count on my acquaintances or friends.

Mother always enjoyed music and dancing. In fact, she was an accomplished accordion player. Many a cold winter Sunday afternoon when we older children were bored, she would make a large batch of popcorn and play songs on her accordion for us. As far back as I can remember, she had a prayer book and prayed the Catholic Mass most every day. We all prayed together at mealtime, and she always led us in bedtime prayers as well. Other than us children, the priority she most valued was her prayer time, and she shared that trait with us as young children. Over the years, that habit has been the backbone for us when the chips were down and life was tough. During years building our Amway business, I did a lot of praying, believing that if I was going to be successful, I would have to do it all myself. I was praying for God's help. I had similar experiences in the early days of building my investment business practice. God always answered my prayers. Sometimes he said, "No!"

"O Mary, conceived without sin, pray for us who have recourse to thee."

MEMBERSHIP CARD

THE CENTRAL ASSOCIATION OF THE MIRACULOUS MEDAL

475 E. CHELTEN AVE., GERMANTOWN, PHILA. 44, PA.

Stanley M. Ree

IS A MEMBER AND FOR ONE YEAR
SHARES IN ALL THE SPIRITUAL BENEFITS.

COPYRIGHT 1958
THE CENTRAL ASSOCIATION
OF THE MIRACULOUS MEDAL

Joseph A. Skelly

DIRECTOR

Membership Card, 1957

Another idea she came up with was for us children to all sit around the dining room table while she taught us Robert's Rules of Order and how to run board meetings. Being the oldest, I always wanted to have the prestigious job of being the president. But, she wanted all of us to experience that role. Throughout the summer, each time we had a board meeting, the roles we played on the board were different. That way, we learned what was expected of us in the president, vice president, treasurer, and secretary positions. Being as religious as she was, she always supported the Miraculous Medal Association in Philadelphia, which was a Catholic organization. She organized some of our meetings around that organization and encouraged us to save any money we could to donate as a family to that organization.

The summer I turned 11, I spent a few weeks at Grandpa and Grandma Reeg's farm. Since I was their first and oldest grandchild, they always treated me special. While I was there, my aunt Arlene Victor came home from her honeymoon in Colorado. Her brother Edwin had arranged a surprise shivaree party at Grandpa's house for them. I had never witnessed anything like that before. The five of us were sitting around the dining room table after dinner when all at once we heard a loud explosion and a lot of banging noise. Well, the explosion was Ed shooting off a 12-gauge shotgun, and the other noise was all of their relatives and friends banging pots and pans together as hard as they could to make as much noise as possible. That was quite an experience! City folks don't know what a shivaree is these days.

In the summer, Grandma was always fond of her strawberries, blackberries, raspberries, and other berries that Grandpa picked. She always looked forward to the Colorado peaches arriving at the Big D Supermarket in Bellevue. On the southwest corner of their two-story farm home was a room that she referred to as her "summer kitchen." On hot days, she would invite Grandpa, Leroy, and me into the kitchen around 3 p.m. for a snack. Generally, it was bowl of large juicy berries or fresh Colorado peaches she served with fresh cream and brown sugar over the top. The summer kitchen was generally used for storage during the winter months.

The other room we rarely spent time in was special as well. She called it the "parlor," and that is where she had a nice fancy sofa and upholstered chairs sitting on carpeting. The room also had some beautiful live fern plants of which she was fond. We were invited into that room only on special occasions. Grandma always had a rather large garden that evolved because she had eight children.

In those days, Grandpa milked a few cows by hand while sitting on a three-legged stool. He didn't have stanchions to hold the cows in place while he was milking them, so he would just sit down on a stool where the cow stood and milk it. At that time, he didn't have a dedicated building for the cream separator, but he did have a small slab of cement where the separator was mounted just outside his tiny tool shed. When my Uncle Perly came home from the Army, he designed and built a larger building with a cement floor, and it had a mounted separator. He also built Grandpa his first machine shed in which to store the little Ford tractor and a few other small pieces of farm equipment.

When we would visit Grandpa and Grandma Reeg's house, we always had something with wheels with which to play. Uncles Eddie and Perly had built a couple of motorized wooden golf cart-style vehicles for us to ride around the farmyard. That may be what started my obsession with cars and speed.

In the spring of 1959, Bobby Weber, Richard Mesch, and I graduated from St. Donatus Catholic Grade School. Bobby went to work as a hired farmhand. Richard and his parents moved to Dubuque, where he attended Senior High School in Dubuque. After much discussion, it was decided that I would attend Marquette High School in Bellevue, even though Dad had to pay $300 tuition there. The next three years, I attended Bellevue High School, a public institution, as it offered free tuition.

St. Donatus Catholic Grade School, 1959 Graduation
Sister Seraphica, Richard Mesch, Bobby Weber, Stan Reeg
Richard Mesch passed away in October, 2018.

When I first attended Marquette High School as a freshman, there were 56 students from many of the local Catholic parishes, like Bellevue, Springbrook, Andrew, St. Donatus, and St. Catherine's, in my class. It was a totally different experience than having three students in my grade school class. I made a fair number of friends but participated only in academics; in other words, no outside sports activities. As a freshman at Marquette, I attended several "sock hops" that were held in the old St. Joe's Grade School gym. There was not a lot of dancing going on, though, as most of the time the girls were standing on one side of the gym, while the boys were all standing on the opposite side of the gym. I had befriended another freshman, Loren Clasen from Andrew, Iowa. His older brother Leo was a senior in 1959 at Marquette, while his sister Janet was a junior.

So, I danced a couple of songs with her at the sock hop, as she was a very good dancer (especially compared to me). I had not really danced in public before, but Mom did teach me a few dance steps so I would have a clue.

After that first year was over, Dad said he was not going to pay $300 for me to attend Marquette, so the decision was made for me to attend BHS #1. Now there were 12 or 14 of us in our class. The number varied depending on who got kicked out of Marquette for behavioral issues and joined us. When I graduated from BHS, there were 12 in my class. I like to joke, "I'm not bragging, but academically I was in the top two-thirds of my class!" There were four girls and eight boys. The only outside activity I ever participated in was being the manager of the high school varsity basketball team one year. Dad always told me that if I wanted to participate in sports, I had better figure out how to get the 10 miles to and from school on my own. Since I was about two years younger than most of my classmates, I was not as mature socially and, therefore, didn't participate in many school functions. I never attended a prom, and I went to the alumni banquet only in my senior year of high school.

Bellevue High School, 1964

Two highlights of my academic experience at Bellevue High School still stand out in my mind. The first was during my junior year when I decided I would enroll in a chemistry class. It was a subject I had been intrigued with ever since we older children received a chemistry set at Christmas several years before. My teacher was Burnell Smith. It was the first chemistry class he ever taught, as he had just graduated from college. I am not sure if it was his inexperience or what, but by the end of the first semester, I received a "D" on my report card, which, for me, was appalling! Needless to say, I did not take chemistry the second semester, as that was the only "D" I ever received in school! But, I have to give Mr. Smith some credit, as he also was our typing instructor. Not only was I as good as the girls in my class, but I earned "straight A's" in typing. And that skill has served me very well over the years, as shortly thereafter was the advent of computers. Many football fans don't know that when Dallas Cowboys Hall of Fame quarterback Troy Aikman was a junior in high school in Henryetta, Oklahoma, he was the Oklahoma state high school typing champion.

When I was 14, Dad decided I needed a summer job, so I went to work for his brother Carly on a farm just a few miles west of St. Donatus. The first year I was paid $90 per month and the second year, $100 per month. Previous to that, I worked on farms for some of our neighbors. It was in the middle of the summer, and I stacked hay bales on the wagon behind the baler, which was pulled down the hayfield by a tractor. If you were really unlucky, you ended up in the haymow of the barn, stacking bales while the elevator just kept dumping more. The chaff and dust rained down on me, and it was at least 110 degrees up in the hayloft. Wow, was that ever hard and dirty work! I hated it, but it was a way to make a few bucks since I never had any spending money. Another positive was building up my muscles in a different way than my grandkids do. Not that I was ever a muscle man—it was not my forte! I am a firm believer in exercising and lifting weights, and for more than 40 years, I ran two to three miles three or four days a week. Now I do some exercises and walk three miles or more at least five days a week.

Working for Uncle Carly was an interesting experience. He had no money when he rented that farm and another farm a couple of miles north of St. Donatus.

Carly was very short tempered, and the farm was all rough hillsides with limestone bluffs in the fields. He would have me cultivate the corn rows to get the weeds out of his crop. Today they use chemicals to do that, plus much of the corn seed today has genetic breeding that limits the impact of worms, weather, and weeds in order to maximize yield. I would be out cultivating and, all at once, I would hit a large piece of limestone. The limestone would break off the shovels on the cultivator mounted to the tractor. Uncle Carly would blow up and yell at me for not being careful enough! It was like it was my fault. But in looking back on the situation, he probably was so frustrated because he could afford to rent only a farm with rough ground like that.

Uncle Carly was milking a small herd of Holstein cows. When he would go out of town, I was responsible for milking the cows. I hated that job. I never knew how long to keep the milk machine on each cow, so I didn't know if I was getting the maximum milk. Later on when my brother Bill was milking, he always got high output from his dairy herd. He fed them properly and knew when each cow reached the maximum output. Most of the work was hard and dirty. Maybe that is why my Uncle Leonard made the comment to me one day when I was staying at his farm for a couple of weeks: "You'll never amount to anything in life because you don't want to get your hands dirty!"

The positive thing about Uncle Carly is whenever he and Aunt Betty were going to church, a wedding, a dance, or out to dinner, he was always dressed very nicely. When I attended Marquette High School the first year in 1959, I had two pair of slacks, black and blue, two shirts, and a pair of black loafers. It is pretty hard to mix them up and make it appear like you had more. So when I worked for Carly that first summer, I saved every penny of my earnings to purchase some decent clothes. Before I went back to school in the fall of my sophomore year at Bellevue High School, I purchased a variety of outfits. Uncle Carly took me to a few nice clothing stores in Dubuque, and I spent some of my hard-earned money on a small wardrobe, including nice black shoes.

Unlike freshman year at Bellevue Marquette Catholic, you could wear blue jeans and a t-shirt at Bellevue High School if you desired. Shoes were a big issue to me because in grade school, I had only one pair of shoes. We boys wore one pair seven days a week unless we were running around barefoot, which is what we generally did during the summer when we were young. Sometimes the soles separated from the upper leather of our shoes! We just put red Ball Mason jar rubbers over the toe and sole of a shoe to hold it together. Embarrassment is a great incentive to work hard!

The summer of 1960, just before my sophomore year in high school, I picked up a bad habit that I thought was cool: I started smoking Marlboro cigarettes. By the time I was back in school in the fall, I was out of money, so I quit smoking, which was fortunate. I never inhaled on purpose, so I was not really addicted. Interestingly enough, when I first met my wife Betty, she was going through the stress of getting through nursing school, and much to my surprise, she and many of her friends smoked. Fortunately for her it, was only a fad and did not become a long-term habit.

> "There is no proof that smoking causes cancer. Well, there's no living proof!"

After many years of my brothers and me being laughed at or bullied by our older peers in grade school, we learned how to use our fists well. My brother Billy still talks about some of the scuffles I was involved in that he witnessed. Generally it would start out with words with each other and then the next thing you know I would lose control of my temper. I would just make a fist and hit the other guy under the jaw as hard as I possible could. That generally ended the fight or argument. Today I'm a little embarrassed to talk about that part of my life, but it is part of what has made me what I am today. At a young age it also taught me not to care or be influenced by what others thought of me. I realize that most everyone who knows me today would find it hard to believe I was that aggressive when I was young!

From those many scuffles and fights, I learned some lessons I've never forgotten. My opponents were generally physically larger than I was. At the time I weighed about 140 pounds. In some cases I could have gotten seriously injured, but I've always been a lucky guy! Maybe some of my angels were looking out for me and protected me from harm? Speaking of angels, as I've gotten older, I believe more in them.

A perfect day in DeWitt, Iowa

Chapter 3

A VISIT TO PLANET REEG

Population 7

FAMILY TIES

Tell 'em Billy Boy Is Here

My brother Billy was born in 1947 in Lancaster, Wisconsin, and Dad was still working for Mom's uncle as a hired man. Dwaine Frantzen, who just lived a couple houses down the street, became a good friend of Billy's. They both were somewhat inquisitive or mischievous, and they always had something going on, as they were full of energy. I remember that Billy seemed to get spanked with the yardstick more than the rest of us older boys. So, all the years we were attending St. Donatus Catholic Grade School, Billy and Wayne (as we always called him) were in the same class. Wayne never attended formal classes beyond elementary school, but don't let that fool you, as he has an engineering mind, is an excellent welder, and can fix any piece of equipment on Bill's farm. In fact, he is innovative to the point that he can make things better than how they were manufactured.

For some reason, Billy moved to Monticello, Iowa, where Mom's sister Delores and her husband Leonard Hosch farmed. They did not have any children, so they invited Bill to live with them. He attended eighth grade and his first year of high school in Monticello. After that, he moved back home and attended Bellevue High School and graduated in May 1965. He dated various girls until February 1965, when he met Diana Nemmers at a teen hop at the LaMotte Knights of Columbus Hall. He was driving my 1956 Ford, so he took Diana home that night, and he asked her out for a date the next night. When he went to leave her house, the car would not start, so Diana's mother helped him push it around the corner so he could coast down the hill and start it. The next evening, he had his first date with Diana.

I did not get to meet Diana until I came back from basic training two months later. All I remember is that the first time I saw her, she was this 5'2" blonde that looked like a doll. And my brother Bill was dating her! Well, he was in love, and a year later, they were married. Later that year, they had their first daughter and named her Kristi. Meanwhile, he was working as a farmhand and doing odd jobs. I was laid off from International Harvester when I came back from my active military duty. I was doing a few odd jobs, but I was partying almost every night. And by December, I decided it was time to get on with my life, and I had heard they were hiring at Farmall in Rock Island. So, I talked Bill into going down with me, and we got hired immediately. We started at Farmall on December 3, 1965. He went to the machine shop, and I went to work in the assembly line area as a tractor repairman. Bill decided he was not going to be a factory worker all of his life, as he really wanted to be a farmer. In 1968, when he was working first shift 7 a.m. to 3 p.m. at Farmall, he decided he needed to start building up some funds. He got the bright idea of also working second shift, from 3 p.m. to 11 p.m. about four blocks down the street at Deere Plow Planter. Sure enough, he got hired the first day he walked into their employment office. The personnel managers and HR people knew that those young men who grew up in the rural areas of Iowa and Illinois knew how to work. He did that for 89 days before Deere cut back and he was laid off. Can you imagine working on a factory floor for 16 hours a day for three months? One thing about us "Reeg boys" is that no one can ever accuse us of being afraid of work!

In September 1968, we were both laid off. Bill went to work as a farmhand for Harold Herrig just west of St. Donatus a couple miles. He was earning the same $120 per week as he did at Farmall, but now he was working 60 hours a week instead of 40. At that time, he started purchasing newborn calves, feeding them milk replacer, and raising them to the point that he could maybe build up a herd. He was thinking about farming for a living instead of working in a factory.

I was in the Army Reserves at that time, and one of my associates was Pat Crippes, who worked in the human resources department at John Deere Dubuque Tractor Works. One Sunday at a reserve meeting, I asked Pat if Deere was doing any hiring at the plant. His response was, "We are hiring, but mostly looking for experienced machine operators." I told him about Bill's background as a machinist at Farmall, and he told me to send Bill in for an interview. Bill went to Deere the next day and was hired after the first interview. He took his physical and went to work as a machinist second shift that evening. The other three guys who got hired that day all went to work in the foundry, which was not a fun place to work. That was the fall of 1969.

Bill continued to work as a machinist at Deere in Dubuque, then in 1970, due to a slowdown, he was laid off again. I was also laid off from Farmall Works (which was the red tractor plant) at that time. As it was, International Harvester in East Moline recalled both of us to work on a special six-week project. Bill drove to East Moline every day for about six weeks. I was living in DeWitt by that time, so I drove in from there. We worked together repairing and updating some components on the IH combine. When that project was completed, we were laid off again.

One of the farms my brother Bill had been renting was owned by Loras Nemmers, who was thinking about selling because farm prices were escalating. Billy told him, "Let me know what you want for the farm, and I'll buy it." It ended up that Loras wanted to maximize the sale price and decided to do a farm auction instead. All of us brothers agreed that we would help Bill buy the farm since he could not afford to purchase it on his own. On the day of the sale, I was in St. Louis for an A.G. Edwards business meeting and not able to be at the auction. So, our brother Mickey flew in from Colorado for the sale. He and Bill sat in the front row of Lombardi's Ballroom, where the auction was being held. The auction company decided to split the Nemmers farm into three components for the sale in order to get the best price.

They split it into the main tillable acreage of the farm in the valley, the hillside and timber, and the land on top of the hill. Billy was primarily interested in the tillable cropland, as that is what he had been renting from Loras. The ballroom was full of people, and Mickey and Billy had the first bid and the last bid. They bought the farm for $6,100 per acre which, at that time, was a record high sale price for a farm in Jackson County. Bill wrote the check to cover the down payment, as we brothers had decided ahead of time that we were helping Billy buy that farm for whatever it took. It was a good farm.

Mom's birthday, December 1998
Don (Red Rocks), Jim (Doc), Judy, Billy, Imelda, Mike (Mort), Stan

After the sale, Billy and Mickey went to Kalmes Store in St. Donatus to celebrate our purchase with all the locals. As you might imagine, there were a lot of nosey people in the auction audience, but only a couple of them were really interested in buying the farm. Everybody was telling Bill and Mick how crazy they were for paying that much money for a farm in Jackson County. So what happened next is quite an amazing story. The next day at 8 a.m., Brian Kalmes, who is the youngest son of Windy and Helen Kalmes and is well connected around the

Tri-State area, rang Bill's doorbell. With Brian was Jonathan, a man who was at the sale the previous evening. Bill did not know Jonathan, but Jonathan was interested in buying the farm from us. He paid us $6,500 per acre and gave Billy three years of free rent on the tillable acreage Billy had been renting previously. We never had to cover the check Billy wrote the night before, and we all made $100,000 overnight! So then everyone in the area told us how LUCKY we were. When we look back on it now, we wish we had kept the farm, as it was very productive acreage, and farm prices accelerated significantly the following decade.

We brothers always appreciated how hard Billy had to work and by this time, the other four of us had done quite well financially, so we wanted to help him. One Saturday morning in September 2008, Billy called me around 10 a.m. He told me his neighbor Pat O'Rourke had just left his place. The reason Pat had visited Bill was that he had nine children and he had his farm in a trust, but he didn't want the kids fighting over the farm after he was dead. A realtor had told him the farm was worth $3,500 per acre, but he would sell it to Billy for $3,000 per acre. Billy told him he'd think about it since it was adjacent to two of the farms he already owned. The next thing Billy did was call me. I told him, "We are going to buy that farm!" He said he could afford only about a 10% stake in the farm. I suggested he call our Colorado brothers to see what percent of ownership they would be interested in owning, and I would buy the remaining interest. As it was a $903,000 purchase, our Colorado brothers (Mickey, Dony, and Jimmy) said they would take one-third of the deal. Bill called me back, and I told him, "Call Pat. Tell him you are buying the farm." I also told him to get a $10,000 earnest check deposit over to Pat ASAP to tie up the deal and to get the closing scheduled with Dan Condon in DeWitt. Bill called Pat back, and we had the farm bought by noon that day before anyone else even knew it was for sale! We closed on the purchase about 30 days later, and I took 31.25%, the Colorado boys took 31.25%, Billy took

25%, and his son-in-law John took 12.5%. We formed an LLC and named the entity Reeg Land & Cattle Co.

In 2008 and 2009, our country was dealing with the financial crisis, and most business owners were feeling the pinch. The construction business got really tight in Colorado, and my brothers needed the money they invested in the farm. So, I bought their 31.25% interest. Now I owned 62.5% of the farm. My intention was not to own the farm, but to help Billy out, as I was not trying to make a big profit on my portion of the investment. By March 2011, Billy had paid off one of his other farm loans, and he was able to borrow the funds to cash me out of Reeg Land & Cattle Co. He paid me 4% annualized interest, and he benefited significantly from rising farm prices. I could not have been any happier for him! I believe Bill's success can be attributed to good business acumen, a lot of hard work, and the fact that he had farmed in other parts of eastern Iowa previously and had learned from some of the best farmers in those areas.

In 2017, much to my pleasure, Bill had another very positive circumstance arise, whereby he would be debt free, own 500 acres or more of quality farm ground, and be in a position to retire at 70 years of age. That's pretty good for a hardworking Iowa boy who started with nothing but a desire to succeed and was willing to work like no other farmer in Jackson County!

The Mick Wasn't Irish

Michael Robert Reeg (whom we called Mickey) was born in 1948 at the Bellevue Memorial Hospital. By that time, Mom and Dad had moved from Wisconsin to a farm home west of Bellevue. Dad had just gotten hired on at John Deere Dubuque Tractor Works where he worked for the next 30 years. He always had good hourly paying jobs that were hard physical work but by that time he was used to it because when he got out of grade school he went to work for neighbors as a farm hand. Furthermore, he had to hand most all of his earnings over to his Mom and Dad. In fact, to the point that when he and Mom got married in August 1945 they did not own a car. So, for their honeymoon they borrowed his brother Bob's car to go spend a few days in Chicago up by the Great Lakes Naval Station where Mom's brother Bob was stationed as he was in the Navy. Bob was at Pearl Harbor on December 7, 1942 when the Japanese bombed the Harbor and all the ships. Shortly after the bombing he contacted Malaria fever and had come back to the States. He also brought with him a beautiful blonde Australian War bride by the name of Connie. By the way, many a U.S. soldiers came back after World War II with a bride from the countries they served in Europe like Germany, Poland, Austria, and Italy. Whenever we ever went to visit them, she always had makeup and lipstick on and with her blonde hair she was the prettiest aunt we had on the Adams side of the family, which was Mom's relatives. Evidently, Bob thought the same as they ended up with 11 children. Bob Adams also was Mickey's baptismal godfather.

Mickey attended St. Donatus Catholic Grade School and Bellevue High School where he graduated in May 1966. The following fall he decided to enroll at Devry Electronics Institute in Chicago where he attended classes for about nine months. During that time he also worked part-time with some of his classmates at the local UPS terminal. Once he quit attending classes he decided to move over to Rock Island where Billy and I lived and went to work in the foundry at Farmall.

Less than a year later he was laid off and moved back up to St. Donatus taking on miscellaneous jobs as he was now A-1 draft status with the U.S. Army. By 1969 he was drafted into the U.S. Army. While in basic training, he and another Iowa boy, Rick Lievrouw, volunteered to go Airborne. After graduating from jump school in Fort Benning, Georgia they were assigned duty at Fairbanks, Alaska at Fort Wainwright. He and Rick were discharged from the Army in early 1971.

Rick's brother Dale lived in Colorado Springs, Colorado so that is where he and Mick settled. They became laborers in the Masonry trade and in June 1972 Mickey began his bricklayer's union apprenticeship program. A year later our brother Dony moved to Colorado and became a union apprentice bricklayer. While they were fulfilling their four year requirement to become a bricklayer they worked for Masonry Contractors during the day and on evenings and weekends they did masonry projects on their own in order to make some extra money.

About this time he met his first wife Deb and they were married March 2, 1974. They had two sons, Justin and Casey whom now live up in Oregon and Washington State. He was divorced in 1978 and met the love of his life Peg Roddy that year. Several years later they were married and she has a son Brian Roddy that lives in Denver. Mick treats Brian as he would his own son.

By early 1976 the two of them had saved $3000, owned a small electric cement mixer, a masonry saw, some scaffold, and a couple of pickup trucks. By now Mick had become a union bricklayer and Dony was finishing up his apprenticeship so on April, 1, 1976 they started their own company and called it Tri Star Masonry, Inc. Our youngest brother Jimmy in 1975 upon graduating from High School decided to join the brothers in Colorado Springs. In 1982 he became a full partner in Tri Star with Mick and Dony.

The first time Mickey was diagnosed with skin cancer was in 2006. He had surgery on his leg and was told he did not need to do chemo or radiation as the doctor thought they got it all. But in the spring of 2009 he was diagnosed with cancer for the second time. He had surgery on the other leg followed by chemo therapy. After four months of chemo treatment he did several radiation treatments as well. He goes in every six months for a Cat-Scan but seems to have remained cancer free since that time. It is scary how many families in America are dealing with cancer in their family. It seems to be epidemic.

Over the past 42 years Tri Star has built hundreds of commercial buildings like schools, churches, Walmart's, Sam's,
shopping centers, and theatres all over Colorado, Nebraska,
Kansas, and other states. They have restored the exterior stone
and masonry on many historical buildings and courthouse
throughout the state of Colorado as well.

The three of them still work a lot of hours like they always have.
They attribute a lot of their success to the values our parents
passed on to us. Those attributes being: common sense, hard
work, fairness, honesty, treating everyone equal, and in the
face of negativity and adversity to just persevere.

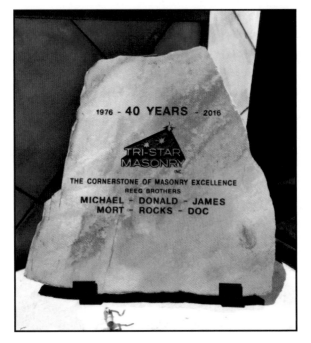

Tri-Star, 40 years, monument in Colorado Springs.

Jimmy (Doc), Stan, Mickey (Mort), Imelda, Judy, Billy, Dony (Red Rocks).

Judy Toots

In 1950, our first sister Judy was born in Bellevue. For some reason, Dad always called her Toots. The stone house we lived in at the time was 100 years old, and it had walls that were 12-inches thick. It had a basement foundation constructed of loosely placed rocks. It was right next to the highway, so when heavy equipment and trucks drove by over the previous years, the vibration disintegrated the stone foundation and walls. The rock walls had cracks in them as much as an inch wide. Needless to say, it was not a very weatherproof house.

Judy attended St. Donatus Catholic Grade School for eight years. She was in the last graduating class of the old stone schoolhouse in 1964. When she was 10 years old, she started babysitting for neighbors' kids. We always thought she was Dad's favorite, but she earned the right. When I became a teenager and was getting ready to go out for a night with my buddies, Judy would always iron my shirt and polish my shoes. She always was trying to make me look good. Fortunately, when I met Betty McCarthy, she was of the same mind-set as Judy.

By the time Judy graduated from BHS in 1968, she already had been working in the office at the high school. When she graduated, she went right to work at the high school administrative office at the new Bellevue High School campus on the west end of town. She had responded to a blind ad in the *Bellevue Herald*, and the superintendent interviewed her and confidentially promised her the job even before she graduated. She worked at BHS until the spring of 1971, when she started at the Dubuque Business Institute as a secretary to the director of the school. Following that, she went to work at Computer Associates in Dubuque, which was a service bureau that did key punch entry work, bookkeeping, and accounting for numerous businesses.

Somewhere along the line, Judy made time to take about 30 hours of accounting classes on a part-time basis at the University of Dubuque. She did a lot of clothes modeling over the years for Beeline clothing, Queens Way, and the Posh Limited in Dubuque. She also did modeling for various charity events. Plus, she is always the first to volunteer for whatever the cause may be. She is a wonderful sister and deserves all the good fortune she gets.

In the spring of 1970, Judy met Ken "Tex" Lochner of St. Catherine, Iowa, and they were married a year later. In the summer of 1973, they built a nice house on some acreage near the top of Crystal Lake Cave Hill.

In October 2000, Judy started doing accounting and bookkeeping for Helen Kalmes at Kalmes Store in St. Donatus. Seventeen years later, she is still working there a day or two a week.

Judy and Ken had three children, with the youngest being a girl born in 1982. They named her Alicia Rae, and she was special— she had tuberous sclerosis. She was diagnosed a few months after she was born. A side effect was that her brain calcified and did not develop. So she was mentally impaired and needed to be monitored all the time. She was a tall girl, and when she was 10 years old, she went to Hills & Dales, which is a home for special needs children in Dubuque. Judy spent time with Alicia every day she lived at Hillsdales over the next 10+ years. Unfortunately, Alicia died from her illness and complications in 2003. Betty and I were with the family when she passed. No parent should ever have to witness a child of theirs dying as a young person.

The new St. Donatus Catholic Grade School. Note the Pieta Chapel on the hilltop behind it.

View of St. Donatus from the south.

Red Rocks Dony, Dony

Brother Donald was born in 1951, attended both Bellevue High School and Marquette High School. In his senior year, he started working at the Pipeline, which was a pipe-coating company just a few miles north of Bellevue. They had a large batch of pipes that had bad coating jobs on the inside, and the diameter of the pipes was maybe 24 inches. Dony, being a small guy, could crawl inside and chip away the coating with a hammer and chisel-like tool. After a few months of that, he realized there had to be a better way to make money. So, after he graduated from high school in 1969, Dony went to work for the railroad as a gandy dancer. A couple of his friends, namely Kevin Budde and Dennis (Doggie) Michaels, hired on at the same time. They were repairing the tracks along the Mississippi River south of Bellevue. This meant they were replacing railroad ties and pounding spikes into the ties with sledgehammers. Imagine the heat and humidity in the middle of an Iowa summer: What hot, humid, dirty, and hard work that was! The railroad runs along the Mississippi River. Their boss hired his nephew to work with them, but the nephew was lazy and never wanted to do anything. So one day when the boss was away, they threw the nephew in the river. Needless to say, when the boss came back, they were fired.

"Check yourself before you wreck yourself."

At some point around that time, Dony picked up a job at Trausch Baking Co. in Dubuque. Since our brother Mickey was in the Army, Dony drove Mickey's 1948 Ford to work. Well, one night he borrowed brother Bill's 1966 Dodge Dart, and started out in Dubuque with his buddies partying and got carried away. Somehow, he lost control of the car on the way home. He ended up in a cornfield, but in the process, he ran the car through a barbed wire fence and scratched the paint all the way down the side. In order to pay for it, Dony had to get a better-paying job. He heard they were hiring welders at the Chrysler Works in Belvidere, Illinois. Fortunately, Dony had learned his welding skill earlier when he was working on the railroad. His intention was to work there only long enough to pay Bill for the car and get the car repaired and repainted. After a year, Dony quit Chrysler and came back to Bellevue. Guess what? He and Cecil Feil went to work for the railroad again as gandy laborers, but they had a different boss. In June 1971 he decided to move to Colorado where brother Mickey was living. He also moved because it seemed like whenever he was in Bellevue, he would get into trouble with the police force due to the normal "Reeg boy" habit of tearing around with cars and drinking alcohol.

Initially when Dony arrived in Colorado, the job market was tight. He picked up a job as a welder and after a few months of that, he went to work for masonry contractors. Then Dony moved to Colorado Springs, where Mickey was working as an apprentice bricklayer. In early 1973, Dony became an apprentice as well. When they finished their four-year apprenticeships, they would become journeyman union bricklayers.

During the four-year apprenticeship, Dony and Mickey were invited to participate in the annual apprentice bricklaying competition in Denver, which was sponsored by the bricklayers' union. The first time he competed, Mickey was in his third year, and he won first place, while Dony got seventh place in the state of Colorado. Dony competed the next two years and won first place. The last year he was eligible, Dony learned a hard lesson about how life really works. The union people from Denver who organized the competition were tired of the top awards always going to bricklayers from Colorado Springs. So what happens is the judges lay black tar paper down on the site where you will be constructing your masonry and brick structure. Keep in mind, there is a time limit to finish the construction that day. They put Dony's construction mat or tar paper over a drain that was two inches out of level. So he laid up the brick structure and it was not level, so he tore it down and rebuilt it. The organizers didn't want Dony to win first place, so they gave him an unlevel surface on purpose

> "If life were fair, there would be no wheelchairs."

knowing it would be much more difficult to construct a level structure. He ended up getting third place, and an apprentice from Denver got first place. This was his first big lesson—that life is not always fair. Even though you may be good at what you do, someone may undermine what you are trying to accomplish. Isn't that the way things sometimes work? If life were fair, there would be no wheelchairs.

When Dony was 24 and Mickey was 27, they started their own company, Tri-Star Masonry. It was the two of them and another guy. In 1976, Dony was awarded his journeyman union bricklayers card. It was not too long after they started their company that Mickey started having serious back issues. He had injured his back as an Army paratrooper in Alaska in the bitter cold winter in 1969. Dony suggested to Mickey that he would run the jobs and crews and Mick could run the office and obtain new projects to grow the business. They started out with a wheelbarrow, a cement mixer, two pickup trucks, $4,000, and a lot of determination. And boy, have they done that! Most people think they were lucky, but what they don't realize is the boys worked 12 to 18 hours a day, seven days a week for many years. They celebrated their fortieth year in business a few years ago and are still going strong!

Dony is proud of all the great structures they built over the past 42 years. But, he is most proud that they have helped many others become successful along the way and have provided well-paying jobs.

Tri-Star corporate headquarters in Colorado Springs, Colorado.

Sylvan

November 21, 1952, was a sad day. We were all excited about having another brother, but that was not to be. Sylvan James Reeg was stillborn. He is buried in the cemetery behind St. Donatus Catholic Church. This was the event that drove Mom to the third nervous breakdown she experienced in her young life.

Imelda

Imelda Louise Reeg was born on October 13, 1953, and we call her Meldi. Shortly after her birth, Mom, then 35, suffered another nervous breakdown. Our warning sign was that she kept complaining about smelling gas, but we had only kerosene oil burners—no natural gas—in the house. It didn't make sense to any of us at the time, but it may have been a weird reaction to the gassing that went on during World War II in Germany, as she continue to repeat that someone was trying to gas her. When Dad came home from work, he evaluated the situation correctly and took her right back up to St. Joseph's Sanitarium in Dubuque, where she was hospitalized again. What we didn't know is that in addition to counseling, she repeatedly received a series of electronic shock therapy treatments. At seven years of age, the thought that I distinctly remember having was, "Will I ever have a normal mother again?" It was a pretty scary time for me and my younger siblings. Fortunately, after six weeks, she came back home. Meanwhile, one of Dad's drinking buddies who formerly lived just north of St. Donatus was now living in Maquoketa. His name was Harry Martin, and his wife's name was Imelda—hence, why our sister was named Imelda. They never had children and they were delighted to take care of Meldi while Mom was in the hospital. In fact, they wanted to adopt her, but Mom thought better than that—she could raise her own daughter!

Meldi attended St. Donatus Catholic Grade School like the rest of us. She graduated from BHS in May 1971. While in high school, she did a lot of babysitting and house cleaning work for hire. After graduation, she worked as a waitress at the Julien Motor Inn in Dubuque and at Sweetheart Bakery.

After divorcing her first husband, Meldi met Troy Budde from Dubuque. He was in the insurance and real estate business. In 1984, they purchased a little gas station in the heart of Key West, Iowa. They converted it into a convenience store and called it Budde Quick Stop. They built quite a successful business of it over the next 10 years. They fell in love and got married in 1985. During the years she and Troy were together, they accumulated a number of rental properties in and around Dubuque.

In 1997, after they separated, Meldi decided to establish a profession and develop some security for herself. She became a cosmetologist and started her own business immediately. She purchased a two-story house in the heart of Dubuque, which she converted into a beauty salon and spa where she had five chairs that she rented out to other experienced beauticians. It was one of the nicest salons in Dubuque. She made a lot of friends and developed quite a successful business.

Unfortunately, Meldi has suffered from depression and mental health issues. We all think we are perfect, but there are millions of people in America who suffer from depression and other mental illnesses. It is a major issue in our society and it goes undiagnosed and/or untreated quite often. As a result of not being able to work every day, Meldi sold the salon in 2014.

Jimmy (Doc)

James Paul Reeg was born in 1957 at Mercy Hospital in Dubuque.

As a youngster, Jimmy worked with Dony and Imelda for an old farmer picking up corn that had dropped on the ground while being harvested. Some of it may have fallen off the picker as it was being harvested, and some may have missed falling in the wagon. They would fill a five-gallon bucket, then dump it in a bushel basket for the farmer to dump it in the wagon. When Jimmy was eight years of age, he started working at a junkyard. When he was 11, he pulled the engine out of a 1958 Chevy. He disconnected everything, including the transmission, but was not strong enough to utilize the chain hoist to lift it out of the engine bay.

Jimmy graduated from Andrew High School in 1975 and moved to Colorado Springs, where two of his older brothers lived. He worked as a hod carrier for seven years and then became a bricklayer. He joined Mike and Don at Tri-Star Masonry as a partner, working seven days a week for years.

Due to all those hours worked, Jimmy saved a little money while Mike and Don kept telling him that he needed to get into the Colorado real estate market. In 1977, Mike's father-in-law had a duplex for sale. Jimmy was able to purchase it. It was great timing as he paid $45,000 and sold it three years later for $78,000. By the time he was 23 years of age, he had accumulated four rental units and the house he lived in. Since that time, Jimmy has been involved in many other profitable real estate transactions

The wedding of Todd and Jodi Reeg. The family on the Springbrook Country Club deck: Dony, Judy, Mick, Mom, Stan, Imelda, Billy, Dad, Jimmy, May 27, 2000.

CURL GIRL: SOMETIMES A WINNER IS A DREAMER WHO JUST DOESN'T QUIT

My brother Dony's daughter, Jacynda Smith, and her family moved from Denver, Colorado, to Bellevue, Iowa, in 2009. Her husband, a professional hockey player, had been injured. She wanted to develop more security for the family and raise her children in a more modest surrounding where she could build a career for herself. Jacynda attended cosmetology school in Dubuque. She would do beautiful curls for many of her customers. She would tell them they could do it themselves at home for free. Most responded with reasons why they couldn't. The main reasons involved curling irons that were on the market at the time.

Jacynda and TYME Iron

She came up with a unique design for a curling iron as well as a straightening iron. She worked with some locals on the engineering and design of it. One of our cousins works for John

Deere in the engineering division, and he helped her fine-tune her invention. It went from concept to an actual model of what it would do and how it would work.

Her three brothers are all involved in this enterprise which is named TYME. There are these four kids, and they have brains. When they get together, they always come up with wild ideas. The four of them have a dynamic that you can't get with most other people. They think outside the box, and they believe they can do anything they make up their minds to do. They had an idea, and they believed in it. They said, "We can take on Clairol. We can take on Matrix. We can take on all the big guns in the hair business and compete with them because we're going to have a better product."

What really made the whole thing was that once they got the design and the prototype built, they continued to refine it. Some of the appliances were manufactured in Colorado, and some were manufactured in Korea. Today, all of it is assembled in Korea, but some of the components are manufactured in the United States.

Not only was it a unique concept that none of the other hair companies had come up with, but they decided to do all initial sales online. They also hired an associate who was good with technology and the Internet. Jacynda did videos of how to properly use the TYME Iron Pro. She did sessions showing people how to use the product, both for straightening as well as curling. They just kept marketing and marketing and marketing. Many of their customers have done online video demonstrations on YouTube. To view some examples, go to TYMEstyle.com. What they've also found is that when they do certain types of promotional ads in a certain way, they get a much larger response than they do through traditional marketing. They keep testing how they can get results on the Internet and get greater sales. It's a remarkable story.

Kierre and Jacynda, founders of TYME

In December of 2012, Jacynda and her brother Kierre filed all the legal paperwork and started the company to manufacture, develop, and sell this product. The company is in Bellevue, where they started out behind a bar in a little storage room. They've since grown to 40 employees. Most of the 40 employees are either living in Bellevue or they're working remote but are originally from Bellevue. TYME has a human resources department. It's like any other company. You have to become more sophisticated. Rather than one or two people making all the decisions and doing the hiring, you need to have an HR manager and a controller. They have a sales department, and Kendrick, Jacynda's younger brother, is the president of the sales division.

They've had China people try to knock them off, but the China product was not of the same engineering quality. Jacynda's two brothers Kendrick and Kierre went online and told the world that those products were knock-offs and were inferior, and they were not TYME's product. They're very tech savvy. They have developed TYME into a company that sells more than 4,000 units at $190 apiece in some months. In 2014, they did $9 million in sales. Last year they did in excess of $15 million in sales, most of which was generated through internet sales.

In the traditional world that I grew up in, I would have never have gotten this company off the ground. It's because these kids were so tech savvy. They knew how to work the market, and that's why they've become so successful. Now they're creating a special kind of hairdryer. It's a totally different development concept than anybody else's, and it's going to last 10 times as long. They've developed cream rinses, shampoos, hairbrushes, combs and all kinds of other products. This is just the base of their business. Now they're doing all these things and becoming a full-blown, real competitive company. It's incredible. I am proud of their ingenuity, creativeness, and most of all, the success they have achieved.

"All for Won, Won for All!"

◇◇◇

——Mickey (Mike) Reeg, brother, Colorado Springs

Part of our mini farm at the Weber stone house was a huge garden that had to be at least an acre. It was so big our Landlord, Verne Weber would plow and disc it up in the spring for us. On summer vacation we all worked in the garden with mainly mom and a little with dad as he worked all week at John Deere. During the summer every morning would start with us listening to Mom read the Catholic Mass out of her hymnal and then we would pray the rosary together. A lot of the days, our Mom along with us, after planting, would hoe around the beans, peas, potatoes, corn, onions, squash, and weed out the strawberry and rhubarb patch for most of the day. So, all summer we had the freshest vegetables, corn, onions and everything from the garden. Mom would also send us out to pick apples, blackberries and gooseberries in the timber-pastures surrounding our house and she would use whatever we brought home to make us pies and jam. We would also put on gloves to go out to cut burning nettles from the nearby pasture which she would boil and they actually were pretty good tasting like spinach to me.

She was an unbelievable cook-baker-hard worker from packing Dad's lunch at five in the morning, making our lunches when we in school, making our meals, baking bread, sweet rolls, sticky bottom rolls, corn bread, taking the produce from the garden and canning it, grating up cabbage to make sauerkraut in the big old crocks, cutting everybody's hair, washing clothes, hanging them out to dry, even in the winter we would come home from school and take down the stiff frozen clothes. She never gave up on anything and was always encouraging us to be the best we could be, as she used to say even if you had to be a ditch digger then be the best ditch digger.

Our dad was also a very hard worker as he went to work every day, whether he had been out late or was sick. All of us kids attribute both of our parent's hard work, attitude, Mom's religious beliefs for our respect of other people, and whatever financial success we have.

We didn't have very many toys but we were very good about entertaining ourselves. Us brothers would roam thru the neighbor's timbers-pastures, make small bow and arrows from trees-weeds, hunt for snakes to kill, go along the small creek trying to catch minnows to eat, and go swimming in the creek where Wayne had taught us how to dog paddle. Some of our cool uncles had motorcycles so we made good use of old tires by rolling them around, making what we thought were motorcycle sounds and pretending the tires were motorcycles. Boy, we've come a long way! Another very adult thing we came up with was swiping some of dad's Pall Mall cigarettes and sneaking into the little log cabin by the garden to smoke them.

All of the time as we were growing up things kept evolving in St Donatus, Runde's Tavern which then became a personal residence, what is now known as the Gehlen House was operated as a bar-grocery store and U.S. Post Office by Roman and Mary Heinricy, then later operated by the Helmle's, purchased as a residence by the Fondell family. Wayne's grandfather Joe Hoffman owned Hoffman's Blacksmith shop where Wayne went to work at right after completing grade school that eventually closed down over the years. Then there was Kalmes Tavern-Grocery-Restaurant (also Feed store at that time) that has been the one constant being almost like a community center for the whole surrounding area. Windy & Helen have owned and operated Kalmes store for over sixty years and have always worked long hours seven days a week. When we were very small and didn't have any money waiting for Dad in their Tavern-Store, Helen would give us an ice cream cone or candy bar. At that age and situation, it was a very big deal. It seems like during our lifetime our family members have had a special connection with their family thru different events and our sister Judy still works for them. It is my opinion that the town can thank God because of the constant presence of the Kalmes' with their unquestionable integrity, character, and commitment. They were the cornerstone of the nice little town of St. Donatus, Iowa!

Kalmes Store

Windy Kalmes and Stan Reeg

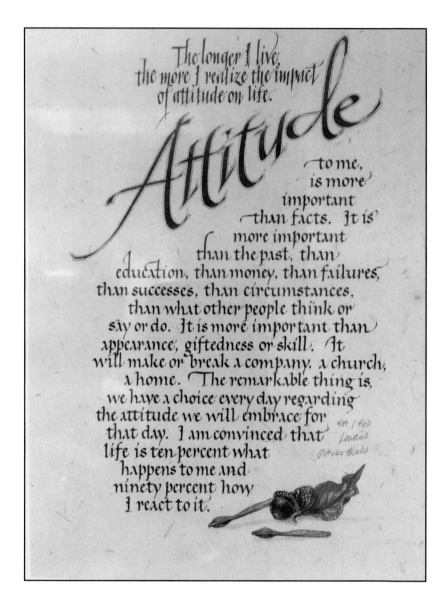

Chapter 4

YOU'RE IN THE ARMY NOW!

Ours?

I found out upon high school graduation that being only 16 years old limited my opportunities. I wanted to attend A.I.C. Business College in Davenport. When I made that suggestion to my Dad, he told me, "You are going to get a job." The issue was I did not turn 17 until two months after graduation. A number of my classmates went to the Air Force, so that is what I wanted to do. Since I was not 18 years of age, my Dad had to sign a release for me to join the Air Force, and Dad wouldn't do that. A few months later, Ronnie Ries, who was a local farm boy and friend of mine, decided to join the Army for three years as Regular Army (RA). He and I talked about it and decided I would go in on the "buddy plan" with him. Again, Dad would not sign for me.

He told me I was going to join the Army Reserves, which is what a fair number of the local farm boys were doing at that time. I enlisted in the Army Reserves in December 1964. I didn't end up in Vietnam, but I was committed to six months of active duty followed by five and one-half years of attending reserve meetings in Dubuque one weekend a month. That didn't seem too bad. Then when Vietnam escalated, the government made our unit a Select Reserve Force, which meant we were required to be at reserve meetings one weekend a month and four Monday evenings a month.

By that time, I was living in an apartment in Rock Island, Illinois, and working at Farmall. It was an 160-mile round trip drive on a two-lane highway to Dubuque and back for the weekly meetings. Plus, every summer we were required to attend two weeks of military summer camp. The first two years were at Camp McCoy, Wisconsin, followed by two years at Fort Sheridan, north of Chicago, and the next two were at Fort Benjamin Harrison in Indianapolis.

In 1965, I was going to basic training at Fort Leonard Wood in Missouri. February 6 was the evening of my "going away party." And boy, did we have a party! It was in the lower level of Pete Runde's bar there in St. Donatus. Once the bar closed, there were six of us that headed to East Dubuque to continue drinking and partying most of the night. Going to East Dubuque was a foolproof plan, and we were the fools to prove it. The next morning, I was to report to Dubuque to catch a bus to Waterloo, Iowa. Since we were partying all night, I missed the bus. So, my buddies purchased another case of beer, and we drove to Waterloo to catch the train to St. Louis.

Basic training was a real eye-opening experience. When we arrived by bus, they took us into a building, and we all were given a haircut, which was basically a butch. I always liked longer-style hair, so that was a disappointment to me. Next, they took us to the quartermaster, where they issued us our military wardrobe. I hate to admit it, but I was not a very good soldier; I resented authority, and we were subjected to that 24 hours a day. The drill sergeants were in control, and we followed orders—or else!

Following nine weeks of basic training at Fort Leonard Wood, I spent the next three months at Aberdeen Proving Grounds in Maryland. My MOS was to be an electronic fuel injection repair specialist. The base was located on Chesapeake Bay, and it was a really scenic place to be stationed. The only negative was that it was a training camp for military officers as well, so any time you were out walking around the base, you were constantly saluting officers.

We did not have to be on duty most weekends, so some of us went to U.S. 30 Dragway in York, Pennsylvania, which was a nationally known drag race facility. We also visited Baltimore and Washington D.C. I don't remember much about Baltimore, as we did a lot of barhopping at night. That was when the discotheque bars were very popular, and we visited our fair share of them! In D.C., we toured many of the historic sites, like the Washington and Lincoln Memorials, Arlington Cemetery, the White House, Congress, etc. I was really impressed with all the large marble buildings. Many years later, when I visited Rome, I realized that many of the buildings in D.C.

were designed similar to those in old historic Italian edifices. It was quite an eye-opening experience for a young man from St. Donatus!

April 1965, Judy, Imelda, Stan, Mom (Marian).

April 1965, Stan Reeg home on leave after Basic Training: Dony, Dad, Mickey, Jimmy, Stan, and Billy.

I came back home from basic training for a one-week leave after nine weeks of training. By then, it was April 1965. As I was flying out of Dubuque to Baltimore for my Army advance training, we flew over downtown Dubuque, and the record Mississippi River floodwaters were surrounding many of the buildings in the south end of town. It was a pretty surreal site! Dubuque is a beautiful city on the Mississippi River, but that spring it was a beautiful city in the Mississippi River. After flying to the Baltimore airport I was shuttled over to Aberdeen Proving Grounds, Maryland, for my advanced AIT training, which was 10 more weeks of active duty. That was a much better experience, as I was in the classroom learning how to be a fuel injection repairman.

Growing up in St. Donatus, we did not have any minorities in our community. About ten years before this, one Saturday morning in Dubuque, Dad pointed eight floors up on the outside surface of a building. There was a hanging walkway and on it was an African-American cleaning the windows. We were amazed that he was hanging out up there cleaning windows. That was the first time we had ever seen a black person.

When I was in basic training, I had a lot of exposure to Negroes, as African-Americans were called in those days, and Native American Indians. Most of it was good. In basic training, we had a nice young man in our company, George Brokenleg from Oklahoma. We became friends. In AIT, I became good friends with another Native American, Gerald Lovelace. He and I visited the historic sites in Baltimore and Washington D.C. on long weekends when we were not on duty. My new minority friends and I attended major drag racing events in York, Pennsylvania. That was about the time the "altered wheel base" drag cars and the "funny cars" were being introduced, so we were witnessing history in the drag racing world.

The highest rank I obtained in the Army was E-4, and it really didn't bother me. After my military experience, I've always had a lot of respect for those soldiers who served us in all the wars and during peacetime. The first three years or so, I was a jeep driver, and at summer camp, I was a deuce and one-half truck driver as well. The latter part of my reserve duty, I was actually an instructor conducting classes on a variety of military topics at weekend duty. The best part of the experience was obtaining an honorable discharge on November 30, 1970.

◇◇◇

Windy and Helen Kalmes celebrating 60 years in business, June 2016.

Chapter 5

LIFE, LIBERTY AND THE HAPPINESS OF PURSUIT

Nurse Betty

Betty McCarthy, 1964

For some reason, I've always felt like a lucky guy. Meeting Betty McCarthy was one of the most fortuitous events of my life. When I got home from my active military duty, I was unemployed for the first few months. Almost all I did was party most evenings with Larry Ploessl. Friday, October 15, 1965, was no different. After Larry and I had a few drinks, he picked up his girlfriend Darlene Weber, and I rode with them to the Dubuque County Fairgrounds for a dance. Even though I didn't immediately recall this meeting the next morning, that evening Darlene introduced me to Betty. All I remember is she was attractive and was there on a date with another guy. I guess I proceeded to hit on her by kissing her like the other guy was not there. The next morning a little before noon, I arrived at Kalmes Feed Store in St. Donatus, and Larry said, "You know, you need to call Betty." And I said, "Betty who?" He explained that she was in a three-year registered nursing degree program at St. Anthony's in Rock Island and that I had told her the evening before I would give her a ride home to Dubuque the following Friday evening. Larry was good at telling stories, so I did not believe him at first. On Tuesday, he finally talked me into calling her and said that he and Darlene would drive me to Rock Island to pick her up Friday evening.

Come late Friday afternoon, I was not too sure about how this evening was going to turn out, so I put a case of beer in a cooler on the back seat, which was pretty common for us in those days. I had a couple of beers on the way to St. Anthony's and, of course, we were late because we got lost in Rock Island trying to find the dormitory. By the time we arrived at the front door of the dormitory, I was pretty apprehensive. They had a break-away plate glass and aluminum door, and there was a young, attractive lady pacing back and forth in front of the door. I gave her an ocular pat down. I said to Larry, "Is that Betty?" And he responded, "That's her." I immediately bounced back with the response, "I am going to marry that woman!" The rest is history because less than a year later (1966), we got engaged after dinner at a supper club in Dubuque. We were married at New Melleray Church by the monastery near Dubuque on September 2, 1967. We held our wedding reception and dance at the fairgrounds ballroom where we initially met. Her Dad Charlie ran a successful trucking business and knew everyone in the area. We had more than 700 guests at our reception, and they consumed a lot of alcohol.

Betty McCarthy and Stan Reeg wedding, September 2, 1967.

Stan and Betty Reeg on their wedding day.

Most Friday afternoons from the time Betty and I met until she graduated from St. Anthony's School of Nursing, I would go to Rock Island to get her and some of her nursing colleagues from Dubuque to give them a ride back home to Dubuque for the weekend. After I hired on at Farmall. I was living in Rock Island, so it was quite convenient for me to give all of them rides to Dubuque.

Betty attended a Dubuque County grade school where she was the only student in her class for all eight years. Going to Wahlert High School in Dubuque, where she had 300 class-mates, was quite a change for her! Obviously, she was bright and had good grades. She also took part in some musicals at Wahlert High School and was a cheerleader.

Betty's father never liked any of the other boys she brought home, but he did not know anything about me, so he had no prejudices when I arrived on the scene. In fact, as the years progressed, he treated me more like a son than a son-in-law. When he died in 1980, I was closer emotionally to him than I was my own father. Charlie died at age 55 from a heart attack.

One of his old sayings was, "Why live to be 100, if you can get it all done in 50?" I believe part of that came from the fact that his father died before age 40 and many of the other males in the McCarthy family died from heart issues at young ages as well. We're all circling the drain faster every day.

The day after our wedding, we opened gifts and headed off on our honeymoon to Colorado. We drove the 1966 GTO west on Highway 30, as there was no Interstate 80 in those days. We visited many Colorado sites such as Pikes Peak, Garden of the Gods, and the Royal Gorge, we viewed the cliff dwellings, and we hiked to Bear Lake in Estes Park.

Betty Reeg snowmobiling on Iceland glacier, August 2018.

Chapter 6

HOW YA GONNA KEEP 'EM DOWN ON THE FARM AFTER THEY'VE SEEN EAST MOLINE?

The Quad Cities: Twice as Nice as the Twin Cities!

FARMALL

After graduating from high school and then turning 17, my Dad told me he found a job for me 12 miles away at Montgomery Ward in Dubuque. Many afternoons and evenings after he got off work at the John Deere factory in Dubuque, Dad would stop at a tavern and drink with the locals, which was a popular thing to do back at that time. Dad told me to go to the Montgomery Ward store in Dubuque on Monday morning and ask for Mr. Mickelson, who was the store manager.

Graduation from Bellevue High School, 1963

Mr. Mickelson had been drinking with Dad at Kalmes' Store in St. Donatus, and he told Dad he was looking for some seasonal help. It paid $1 per hour—good pay back then! I did not have to interview. I just filled out an application and was put to work as a receiving clerk on the dock. When merchandise was delivered to the store, I checked it in and put it in the appropriate area in the storage area of the building.

Everyone who's old enough remembers what they were doing on November 22, 1963, the day President John F. Kennedy was killed. I was working in the store when we heard the announcement on the radio. It was a surreal experience, hearing that someone had killed the President of the United States! The whole nation was in a state of shock for many days following his assassination.

Around Christmas time, I was let go of my job because the holiday retail season was coming to a close.

Then, in early March of 1964, I heard that some of the local boys from LaMotte, a town near St. Donatus, were getting hired at the International Harvester factory in East Moline, Illinois, which was 80 miles away. I drove to the plant to apply for a factory job, and I was hired. The only problem was that I couldn't pass the eye exam. They informed me that I needed to get my eyes examined and needed glasses. I went to Drs. Yohn and Edwards in Rock Island, Illinois. Years later when I got involved in Amway, Dr. Raymond Yohn and his wife became good customers of mine. And Dr. Edwards is another story. In my early days in the investment business, I stopped at the Maid-Rite restaurant on Fifth Avenue in Rock Island for lunch, and Dr. Edwards was sitting on the stool next to me at the counter. He was curious about me, as I was wearing a suit, so he asked what I was doing for a living. I told him I had become a financial advisor at Dain Bosworth in Davenport. He told me he and his wife were not happy with their E.F. Hutton advisor, so we scheduled a time to meet. Now, three decades later, Dr. Edwards has passed, and his wife Iris is in her 90s; she is still a very good client of mine.

Once I got my glasses, I reported to work in the factory on March 16, 1964, and I was only 17 years old! My first job was as an inspector at the end of the beet harvester assembly line. I connected the harvester to a power takeoff on a large horsepower GE electric engine that was mounted on wheels so it would be portable. I cranked up the RPMs like you would in the field when it was connected to the tractor. I was checking to see that it functioned properly at operating speeds and to make sure it was properly assembled. Bolts and nuts would fall out on the floor quite often, and I had to determine if they were extras, dropped during assembly, or had fallen out because they weren't properly installed. The plant manufactured that run of harvesters for only four months, then the assembly line was changed over to manufacturing corn planters. On that line, I was assigned to assembling the corn heads for the planters. I found it to be a tedious, boring job, but I was being paid $2.67 per hour, which was pretty good pay in those days.

I knew some of the guys were from my home area, so we established a carpool. There were five of us, so we would each drive one day per week. We were all young guys and made a game out of seeing who could get us to work or home in record time each day. It was 80 miles and all two-lane highways. We did a lot of dangerous, stupid driving and passing of other cars. They say your car is a reflection of your personality. I didn't have a car. So I drove Dad's new 1964 Plymouth.

Around the end of the year, production slowed down, and I was laid off, which was a pretty common occurrence in the agriculture industry in those days. I began drawing unemployment and started going to Army Reserve meetings, as I had enlisted in December 1964.

When I arrived back home from my active military duty in late June 1965, I was still laid off from IH in East Moline, so I started drawing unemployment again and hanging out. Which means that most nights I was out partying, drinking, and sleeping until noon the next day. In those days, Helen Kalmes' brother

Larry Ploessl was living with her and Windy. Larry was managing Kalmes Feed Store at that time. He graduated from LaMotte High School in 1964 and was my age, plus he had a brand new red 1964 Chevrolet Impala, two-door hardtop, and he liked to party, so we became fast friends.

By late fall, I was getting a little bored with that lifestyle, and I heard that International Harvester Farmall Works in Rock Island was hiring. I talked my brother Bill into going with me to see if we might be able to obtain jobs. Bill graduated from high school a few months earlier. We both got hired on the spot. He started out in the machine shop, and I started out in the tractor assembly area as a tractor repairman. I was repairing things that were not properly assembled or components that some assembler didn't get enough time to install. Farmall was building two hundred tractors per day at that time, so we had only about two minutes to install our parts. Then the conveyor would move the tractor on down the line for the next parts to be installed.

Bill and I then looked for a place to live, as we decided we weren't going to drive 160 miles round trip every day. We rented a second-story apartment just diagonally across the street from the Farmall plant, immediately next to the railroad tracks. And boy was it a dump! We thought we grew up impoverished, but this was another thing!

The first thing I did after getting hired at Farmall was to join the Farmall Employees Credit Union. I started saving money out of each weekly paycheck. After you worked 90 days, the Farmall Credit Union would loan you money to purchase a new car. At that time, my Dad's youngest brother Leroy was into Pontiacs and drag racing. I decided I would purchase a new 1966 Pontiac GTO. The list price was $3,450, and I negotiated a purchase price of $3,050. I have always been a tough negotiator when it comes to purchasing cars because I felt that I worked harder to earn my money than any car dealer I ever purchased a car from! It took about six weeks for the car to be built, and it was delivered to the dealer in June 1966. The day the car arrived at the dealership, the sales manager called to confirm that I still wanted the car, as he had two other buyers that were willing to pay him full list price for it. I told him I had been waiting for six weeks and was committed to the purchase.

Stan Reeg's first new car, a 1966 Pontiac GTO.

Man, did I have a lot of fun with that car! It was a two-door hardtop. It was Barrier Blue, with a color-matching interior, and it was fast! I ran it at the dragway in Cordova, Illinois, a couple of times, but I had a lot more fun drag racing other gearheads on the roads around Dubuque and Bellevue. Uncle Leroy was working the second shift at John Deere in Dubuque at that time, so some evenings he would leave work at 7 p.m. and take the remainder of his shift off. Since he knew the guys around there who had the hot cars, like the SS 396 Chevelles, GTOs, 390 Fords, and some Mopars, he would arrange competitions for me. We would go to the designated area on John Deere Road in Dubuque and pair them off. Of course, we always had a case of beer in the car. You have to remember we were the beginning of the Baby Boomers, so there were a lot fewer cars on the road than today. Also, the law enforcement officials were much more lenient, so if they caught us drag racing on Deere Road, they would give us a warning: "If you are caught drag racing again this evening, you'll be in big trouble!" When that happened, we would just head down south of Dubuque to reconvene our drag racing at Zoller Flats.

After a while, I got really bored with working in the assembly and tractor repair area, so I thought I would move to a better-paying job. That meant I would have to go into the machining area and because of my lack of seniority, I would be working nights. I found the best-paying jobs in the plant were in the finish precision grinding area, so that is where I looked to transfer. I ended up bidding for and transferring to a job in Department 34, and I worked in that area most of the next 12 years I was at Farmall. Department 34 not only had the best-paying jobs in the plant, but the union steward, chairman of the grievance committee, and local union president worked in that department. Needless to say, it was a strong union department and if one of the machinists came in with a hangover or didn't want to work that day, they would just walk off the job for the day. It was pretty crazy for me having come from a rural area where you worked no matter how you felt. When there was work to be done, you did it. If no one else could run his machine, the next thing you know, the whole assembly line production would be shut down because they didn't have the necessary parts to complete the assembly of the tractor. Then management would send all the assembly line employees home until the next day.

International Harvester Farmall

We had a lot of "walkouts" or "unauthorized work stoppages" in those days. When our union contract was up for renewal and negotiations, the union decided to strike rather than compromise with the company. Archie McCardell was the chairman of the board of International Harvester and decided he was going to break the union. After being on strike for six months, it ended up that what he really did was bankrupt the company. We were bought out by J.I. Case shortly thereafter. Once the J.I. Case top management reviewed each of the IH operating companies, they decided to close the Rock Island Farmall plant. They moved the main conveyor line to Racine, Wisconsin, where J.I. Case was operating in an inefficient facility that was more than 100 years old. But to them, it was better than having to deal with all the union issues in Rock Island!

Winter of 1979-80 strike

Once the sale was announced, we were all made aware that we would be losing our jobs. It was pretty scary. Here I am, only 38 years of age, with 21 years of seniority at I.H. in East Moline and Farmall in Rock Island. I had never graduated college or developed any skills other than working at Farmall. To make extra money on the side, I had done some carpentry, house remodeling, and interior and exterior painting of houses and garages. I also had the Amway experience and selling real estate with Ralph and Chuck Green in DeWitt, Iowa, my adopted new hometown. Keep in mind that all the years I was working at Farmall, I was always doing something else on the side, so basically I was working two jobs.

In the first couple of years I worked at Farmall, I attended college classes at Blackhawk Community College in Moline. Over those years, I obtained about 24 hours of credits attending classes on a part-time basis. I also took some correspondence classes from the University of Iowa, which I never completed.

My first reaction to the plant closing was shock. It was 1985, and the following fall, my oldest son Todd would be going off to college. Working in the factories was cyclical work. About the time you built up a little savings, you would get laid off again and spend all your savings to meet your family's living expenses. The end result was that Betty and I had not saved one dollar toward our two boys' future college education expenses! Furthermore, we had decided that both of our boys would be getting four-year degrees, no matter what. So Betty decided to go back to work full-time as a registered nurse.

When I was working at Farmall in the early 1970s, we had a janitor who was a very interesting guy. He had some higher education, but he worked in the maintenance division at Farmall, which didn't require a lot of motivation or energy. He was pretty smart book-wise, and was investing in penny stocks at that time.

Many investors who aren't sophisticated think they can buy thousands of shares at pennies a share and someday they will get rich. Obviously, I was looking for all the ways to get rich myself. I was always looking for ideas. I did some penny stock trading through a discount broker myself.

Then I thought, "I can make more money if I buy high-quality companies." Three years later, I met another guy in my department who was investing in oil and gas stocks. He was bragging about how well he had done. I figured that made sense. He was using a broker named Jay at the Moline, Illinois, Robert W. Baird office. I thought, "Well, I'll stop by there and visit with Jay on the way home some afternoon."

One day, I stopped by the Baird office and met Jay, the branch manager at the time. I had sold one of my apartments in DeWitt, and I had $25,000 to invest. He sold me on the idea that oil and gas stocks were really hot and that I should just invest all the money in three oil and gas company stocks. One of the companies was Mesa Petroleum, which was managed by T. Boone Pickens. He was quite prominently followed and quoted in the energy field. The other companies I bought were Worldwide

Energy and Mitchell Energy. I don't believe I'll ever forget those names. After the first month, we received our statement, and we were up 10 percent in one month. I told Betty, "See, I told you we were going to get rich by investing in the stock market." She looked at me like, "Who are you kidding?"

Everything goes through cycles, and that was the peak of the oil and gas stocks in that cycle. All three of the stocks went down significantly in value, and I never heard from Jay again. Years later in the 1980s, he married a second time, and his stepson became a client of mine when I was a Dain Bosworth advisor.

> "When we get all the way back up to broke, we're gonna throw a party."

Jay actually transferred my account to a rookie advisor who never called me either. So I transferred my securities account to Ameritrade, which was a discount broker in Chicago. Over the next three years or so, I sold each of those stocks as they got back to breakeven. It didn't turn out to be a very positive investment experience, but it was a wonderful learning experience. When I got in the investment business in the mid-1980s, I knew one thing: When the markets are down or when a client's investments are down, they want to hear from their advisor. It's an important principle I have never forgotten.

When the markets are running strong and everything is going up, clients are not too worried about hearing from you. But when we see a correction or a sell-off in the market, they want to hear from you because they value your opinion or need reassurance that they are going to be okay.

Those experiences all happened while I was still working at Farmall. We had some interesting characters working at the plant. If you grew up in rural eastern Iowa or western Illinois, many of your neighbors who did not work at John Deere or International Harvester, thought you were really lucky. On the surface, it appeared you were lucky because you made a good hourly wage, had several weeks of vacation per year, and continued to build job security as you built more seniority. You also had fully paid health care insurance, sick leave, and personal days. The reality was that you had a lot of time off because of downtime. All your neighbors thought you had it made.

What they didn't realize is, everything in life exacts a price. The price is that when you're in manufacturing like we were in Farmall, whether you're running a machine or you're an assembler, day after day, week after week, year after year, you are repetitively doing the very same mechanical activities—much like a robot. Maybe that is why a lot of our labor force has been replaced with robots.

For many, it's a very boring way to make a living. We had a few college-educated teachers who gave up teaching because they were not making very good pay compared to factory workers. We actually had several teachers working with us on the assembly line. It was an interesting mix of people, and many of them had nicknames. With some, we didn't even know what their real names were. We had guys named Four Eyes, Alabama, Three Fingers, Fat Boy, etc.

Talking about characters, the first supervisor I worked for at Farmall was Wilbur Catour. He was a hyper person and quite religious. In fact, he was doing some kind of ministry work when he was working at Farmall. He was a nice guy, but a lot of the workers in our department picked on him and messed with his mind. We had one guy who would call him up at midnight or 1 a.m. just to wake him up and aggravate him. There was a lot of juvenile behavior, but I did not participate in that. An interesting side note is that the guy who called Wilbur during the middle of the night ended up getting murdered by his own son when his son went crazy!

Once new employees got beyond a 90-day probation period, they were eligible as members of the Farmall Employee Credit

Union to borrow money for new cars. Many of us young guys had nice new cars.

This included Dennis Pauley, who had a new Oldsmobile 442 and worked in our department. After Farmall closed, he went to work for Iowa-Illinois Gas and Electric. Many years later, he was the mayor of Rock Island.

Another person I worked with was Jeff Leach. Being a car fanatic, I really enjoyed him, because he had a 1936 Ford Anglia two-door sedan, which is an English Ford. He had installed a Corvette engine in it and had very small tires on the front and really wide tires on the back. Sometimes when he was leaving Farmall, he would crank it up and lift the front wheels off the pavement. I wondered, "How did he have enough money to buy that kind of toy?"

George Kutsunis was working on the assembly line with us. George always wore a white short-sleeved dress shirt. At first, everybody thought that was pretty peculiar until we found out that he actually owned a dry cleaners. He was just trying to prove he could clean anything out of a shirt at his cleaners.

Another person I met in the very early days of working at Farmall was a young man, Joe Tree. He had just finished his tour of duty with the U.S. Navy, and he had a few tattoos. He was a wild man. He loved to party, play cards, carouse, and drink. I got to know him pretty well. Many mornings, especially after his Thursday night bowling league, he would come in before the shift started at 7 a.m. on Friday. We had wooden pallets that were probably 40-inch square boxes and about 25-inches tall. They were used when in-bound purchased parts were shipped to Farmall. Joe would crawl in one of those boxes and cover up with a 3 by 4-foot sheet of cardboard that separated the layers of the instrument panels or incoming components that had arrived in the box. He would pass out until the 7 a.m. whistle would blow. Then, he would jump up out of the pallet boxes and go to work.

One of the other primary reasons employees liked the Farmall and John Deere plants at that time was that the United Auto Workers union had negotiated programs with these companies whereby employees could retire after 30 years. The union slogan was, "Thirty and Out." It didn't make any difference what age you were: Once you had 30 years of employment at the factory, you could retire.

I have a longstanding investor, Steve, who has been with me since back in the mid-1980s. When he was young and a new client of mine, he told me, "I plan to retire when I get my 30 years in." He started working at John Deere when he was 18. When Steve turned 48, he retired from the photography department at the Deere Administration Center in Moline.

Steve and his wife did not have any children. Since he always planned to retire after 30 years with Deere, the most important thing for him was making sure we didn't lose a lot of money. His goal was to grow his retirement plan assets and IRAs so he would be able to retire at 48. Steve has always been one of my "raving fans," and he has referred many, many clients to me. Now, Steve has been retired for more than 19 years.

I also have a number of friends and clients who are in their 70s and still working.

The main point I am trying to make is that there are a lot of people in our country who are still working into their 70s. It's not that they all need the money. Many times, they are just ambitious people who have a lot of energy and love what they're doing.

While I worked in that department, I made a number of good friends. One guy who ran a machine by me was named Bob. After the Farmall plant closed, Bob went to work at the Rock Island Arsenal as a machinist. Shortly thereafter, he won $4 million in the Illinois Lottery. He quit his job at the Rock Island Arsenal and moved his family to California. I've not ever heard anything of him since.

International Harvester Farmall, 1980

International Harvester Farmall Plant, 1980

In those early days when I first started at Farmall, production really picked up. They were producing a new model tractor, and they added a second shift. I volunteered to go on second shift because I was able to obtain an easy job in our department. I was assembling the gauges, cigarette lighters, ignition switches, tachometers, and several other components in the dash and instrument panels.

I worked with quite a few nice people, but one of the guys, Ralph, who transferred into our department was very disruptive. He was creating havoc all the time. You could say he was a jerk and had "bad karma." He started snapping me in my privates with a wet shop towel, which really stung. It was juvenile behavior on his part, but he was someone who really needed the attention, and he thought it was funny. He continued to do it to me on a regular basis. One night I told him, "You do that to me one more time, and I'm going to knock you on your ass!"

Of course, he did it again. I told him, "You SOB, I'm going to kick your ass when we get off work tonight. I'll be waiting for you outside the gate." After I made that comment, I thought, "I've got to back my words up." I proceeded to walk around the department, both up and downstairs, to inform the guys what was up. Ralph was 220 pounds and 5'6" tall. He was stocky and looked like a professional boxer or wrestler.

"Hit first, hit fast, hit hard, and hit last."

I decided to settle this matter once and for all because I was tired of his childish behavior. He was as strong as an ox and could kill me. I lined up several guys to protect me if things got out of control.

That night when the shift was over, we all hurried out of the tunnel to the exit gate. I was out there promptly. Earlier, I told my buddies, "Make sure you're there as soon as we get off the shift." So finally, here comes Ralph, walking out of the gate like the big bully he was. When he got close to me, he started running off his mouth like he always did. Finally, after a few minutes of listening to that, I told him, "I've had enough of your bullshit" and I made a fist and hit him as hard as I possibly could right under his jaw. Fortunately, I didn't break his jaw, but I sure shocked him! There was a fight, and thank God Ralph came in second. No autopsy, no foul.

Immediately after I hit him, I felt bad about it. I didn't say anything. I just left him standing there stunned and walked over to my car and went home. Everyone else just walked away peacefully. There was a pretty good crowd of people who heard him running his big mouth off at me, and they observed the end result. Everyone quietly departed and that was the end of the issue for me, as I never had any more problems with him again! Years later, I heard he died from cancer. It did not surprise me, as those kinds of things happen when you have bad karma. The only kind of karma you want in your life is good karma!

I still get fired up telling that story 50 years after the incident happened. I don't know how people can be that stupid, but there are a lot of bullies in our world and they make life miserable for many people around them. It happens at all levels of our society, especially in elementary and high school. It's a big problem, and it leads to a lot of suicides.

Brother Billy's Farmall Turbo 1206 tractor.

Chapter 7

ONCE UPON A SMALL TOWN

I Love Those Dear Hearts and Gentle People in DeWitt

I was working at Farmall in the summer of 1966. The repairman in my area was Homer Martin. Homer was a very interesting guy. He was bored with working at Farmall, so he played in a country and western band on the weekends. During the weekday evenings, he was always busy rebuilding and repairing foreign cars. In 1966, that was a foreign idea…1966 to 1970 was the height of the American muscle car era.

Homer knew that I had bought a new 1966 Pontiac GTO. At the same time, he knew one of the young tractor repairmen downstairs, Dave Bauer, who was from DeWitt, Iowa. Dave had purchased a 1966 SS 396 Chevelle with a four-speed transmission. The older guys decided, "We should be racing those cars." They encouraged us to drag race those cars to see which one was the fastest. Of course, Dave and I didn't need a lot of encouragement. When the evening for us to race came, I drove out to DeWitt.

We went out in the country and lined up the cars. Other people, with a '57 Chevy, Corvettes, an Olds 442, etc. We designated one guy to be the flagman when it was time to take off. When he dropped the flag, Dave and I shot off the starting line with engines revving and tires squealing like crazy. We ran the whole quarter mile nose-to-nose, but I beat Dave's Chevelle by about one fender length. I never really bragged about it because Dave was the reason I was out there, and it was his home turf. We never raced each other again.

That evening after everyone finished drag racing, some of us started drinking and partying. They cut open a watermelon and poured whiskey on half of it. Then they sliced it apart, and we ate whiskey-soaked watermelon. Of course, we were drinking beer at the same time. That's the one and only time I have ever done that in my life. It never did sound very appealing to me. From that point on, Dave and I became fast friends.

When we were at Farmall, Dave was dating Donna, a nice young girl from DeWitt. I had just started dating Betty a few months before that. We ended up getting to know Dave and

Donna very well. I found out that previous to working at Farmall, Dave had been a bricklayer and did masonry work. He later became a part of the skilled trade shop at Farmall as a union bricklayer.

Since Betty and I were originally from the Dubuque area, there were times on weekends when we were driving that 90-minute drive back to Rock Island from Dubuque when we would speculate, "Wouldn't it be nice to live in DeWitt?"

In early 1969, Dave and Donna purchased a lot in DeWitt, and we purchased a lot immediately across the street from them. They decided to build their house right away, but Betty and I decided to wait another year to build ours. We planned to save more for a bigger down payment. The agreement was I would go out the 20 miles and help Dave build his house, and the next year, he would help us build ours. Many a day I drove out to DeWitt from Rock Island in the summer and fall of 1969 to help Dave build their house. He always told me, "You help me with our house, and I'll help you with yours when you build."

When we began the process of building our house in 1970, Dave was a great help. He staked out the lot and after the basement was dug, he poured the footings and foundation. He laid up all the cement block walls, laid the brick for us, poured all the cement, including the basement floor, the garage floor, the back patio, the driveway, and the sidewalks. Dave saved us a lot of money and was a huge help to us, and became a great friend in the process!

After we got married, Betty was working as a registered nurse in intensive care and coronary care at St. Anthony's Hospital in Rock Island. We decided we would live on the money I made at Farmall and save what she was making as a nurse. When we finished the construction of the house, we had a total of $26,000 invested and had to borrow only about $16,000. With my parents never having owned a home in their whole life, taking out that loan was a huge leap of faith for me.

That is the story of how we ended up in DeWitt. We had laid out the house footprint and staked out the basement on April Fool's Day, and on September 1, we moved into the house. It was a fast-track project.

DeWitt has been a great place to raise our boys, Todd and Eric. Eric was born in 1972. He was a very active baby from the beginning and has always had a lot of energy. When we completed the house, Todd was only two years old, and he could barely see out the front windows. Today he is 49 years old. They've always had great schools in DeWitt. We sent the boys to St. Joe's Grade School. During those years, Betty did a lot of volunteering at the school in the library and in the classrooms. She also helped transport and chaperone children when they had field trips.

> "Who are these boys and why are they calling me 'Dad'?"

Both boys attended DeWitt Central High School and ran track and cross country. Todd went to State in both of those fields and to the Drake Relays in 1985. Both of the boys played basketball at St. Joe's and really enjoyed those experiences, as did Betty and I. It was fun watching. It was great entertainment, and it was a wonderful experience for them and helped them build self-confidence.

When it was time for Todd to attend college, a number of coaches were recruiting him because of his success in track and cross country. Loras College in Dubuque was really recruiting him, and they strongly encouraged him to visit, which he did. He visited several colleges and universities, but once he visited the University of Northern Iowa in Cedar Falls, he came home and announced, "That's the school I'm going to attend." That was the year before the plant closed and I lost my job at Farmall. I had just started my career as an investment advisor at Dain Bosworth in May 1985.

Working at Farmall provided unstable and cyclical employment. It meant you would work for about six months, and then you'd be laid off again. Betty and I had not saved a dollar toward the boys' college educations. It seemed like we just started to accumulate some money in savings, and then I would get laid off again and be unemployed. Then we would spend all of our cash reserves.

Betty went back to work full-time when Todd went off to college. That is how we funded the college experience for our boys.

Earning part of their college costs was a good experience for the boys. I went to college on a part-time basis but never completed enough classes to obtain a college degree. So for Betty and me, it was a priority for Todd and Eric to obtain college educations.

Eric was four years younger than Todd. He loved to play golf and was on the high school golf team. He also played basketball during the years he attended St. Joseph's Grade School. He didn't play in high school, but he ran track. He didn't have the competitive drive that Todd did when it came to running. It still was a good experience for him, though. When it was time for us to look at colleges for Eric, he decided he was going to attend the University of Colorado in Boulder. He figured he could go to Colorado where my brothers lived and be close to the mountains and be able to do a lot of skiing the Rockies. Eric is a very bright individual, and he decided he was not going to attend the same college his brother had attended. Interestingly enough, the spring he graduated from high school, he decided to attend the University of Northern Iowa. I don't know why he chose to go there, but he found it to be a great experience. That's where he met his wife in his senior year of college. They've been married 22 years now. So I would say for Eric that it was all a good experience!

Eric and the former Tracy Ripperberger were married in Lacona, Iowa in 1995. They have two children, Trevor and Hanna. Since Trevor is our only grandson, we are hopeful that someday he will have children to carry on the Reeg name for our family.

Todd, Eric, Stan, and Betty Reeg.

Today, Eric always has a construction project going on for relatives and friends. He is quite talented in designing, engineering, and constructing many different types of wood bookcases, bars, cabinets, etc. A few years ago, they built a new home at Echo Valley Country Club in Norwalk, Iowa. He designed and finished out the entire lower level with a bedroom, bathroom, Murphy bed, a game room with a bar, and an old-style 1950s theater with a projector and a 95-inch screen. He and Tracy have excellent jobs at Principal Financial in

Des Moines. He is a pension takeover specialist in their large employee retirement plan area, and Tracy is a mutual fund portfolio manager for Princor Funds on a number of their fixed income mutual funds.

After I was laid off from Farmall back in the early '80s, I worked for Bill McGarry and Charlie Trimble. They were brothers-in-law who lived in DeWitt and owned a successful housing construction business. I had done some work for them, like laying sod, painting, varnishing, etc., on the new houses they were building. By 1986, Charlie was working as an accountant, plus he was running the family farm and trying to complete an 80-acre development called Timber Creek near DeWitt. In other words, he was burning the candle at both ends. Anyway, Charlie and Bev invited Betty and me out to their house in the country for a July 4th picnic they were hosting.

When I was visiting with Bev, she asked me how I was doing in the investment business. I proceeded to tell her how I was cold calling and the success I was having. I also told her that Charlie couldn't keep burning the candle at both ends. He had an accounting and business background, so I suggested that Charlie could be successful in our business. I told her, "You know, if he would ever want to consider the investment business as a career, I could introduce him to Jack Stengel at Dain Bosworth and get him an interview."

After a few weeks and a couple conversations with Charlie, he decided that might be worth pursuing. I introduced him to Jack Stengel, and he went in for an interview. At that time, Dain Bosworth had the same type of profiling and scoring system they had when I was hired. They gave prospective employees psychological exercises that contained 400 questions—basically, it was a personality profile exam. They were looking at how honest you were, what your work habits were and what your loyalty factor was. Charlie was very bright, and with his background, he scored well on the test. Jack Stengel offered him a position, and he accepted.

About the same time, I'm not sure why, but his brother Pat Trimble went to work as a rookie advisor at the local Shearson office in downtown Rock Island. He went through their training program, and in October 1987 when the stock market crash hit, it negatively impacted many new advisors' careers. Pat was not receiving a lot of coaching or mentoring over at Shearson. So Charlie and I convinced him to move his practice to Dain Bosworth, which he did shortly thereafter.

Pat and I became fast friends. He came up with the idea of networking with CPAs and attorneys and doing lunches or breakfasts with them. Since I was a member of Springbrook County Club, I started inviting people to play golf with me there. Generally, I would invite maybe a prospective client, an existing client, and an attorney, accountant, or CPA to be my guest. My goal was to not golf by myself, but to have some business-building potential guest golfing with me. My golf game got faster each time I got my ball retriever regripped.

When I spent the summer of 1985 in Minneapolis going through training classes for Dain Bosworth, Betty joined Springbrook Country Club in DeWitt. Over the years, I have entertained many of my clients on a round of golf along with a social hour and fabulous meals at the Club.

The world around us is changing at a rapid pace, and that means the old paradigms are being replaced. The result is that small-town country clubs cannot continue to use the same business models they've used for the past 50 years. I find time to play golf with a great group of fun guys most Wednesday afternoons in the summer. The real fun begins when we get in the clubhouse and start playing Euchre. We are all very competitive and want to win—just like being a child again! This leads to one of the comments Betty always makes: "Why don't you grow up?" My response is generally the same: "Why would I want to do that?" Aging is a high price to pay for maturity!

We have been blessed with wonderful friends in almost 50 years in DeWitt. Two of our favorites are Mike Devine and Dan Macumber.

Mike Devine grew up in Dubuque. Mike's father died when Mike was in the sixth grade, and his mother died when he was a senior in high school in 1969.

The first job Mike had out of college was with the Jewel-Osco drugstores. After four years of living in five states and traveling all the time, he and his wife Judy decided in 1977 to move to DeWitt, where they lived just around the corner from us.

When they lived in DeWitt, Mike became a good friend of Dan Macumber. Dan worked for Ralston Purina for about 35 years in various roles. I will never forget the night we met Dan and his wife Carol at a St. Joseph's meeting. That was where all of our children went to grade school. We became good friends. Dan had the type of personality where he made most everyone feel like he was their best friend, which he certainly was to me.

At the same time, Father Conrad, the pastor at St. Joe's Catholic Church, made a point to get me into the Knights of Columbus in DeWitt. Not long after that, Dan and Carol arrived in DeWitt. Dan and Dan Gisel, whom we called Gissy, became fast friends and were pretty much inseparable. It was like they were each other's "sidekick."

Dan Macumber loved playing games, especially cards and golf. Dan was a member of the fabled 1960 graduating class of Assumption High School. Both Dans ended up joining Springbrook Country Club in DeWitt. We played a lot of Sheepshead and Euchre games at Murf's Tap and the Knights of Columbus Hall in DeWitt in those early years.

Most afternoons when we finished golfing, we would go to the nineteenth hole and play some very exciting games of Euchre. Dan Macumber was always very lucky at cards, especially Sheepshead. He loved winning, but he was not lucky in life. He died unexpectedly in his sleep at the age of 59. It was a heart attack. By that time, Dan and I were best friends. Dan also organized most all of our couples' and men's social golf outings for our group. Every July, we couples would go to various golf courses or resorts in northwest Illinois, eastern Iowa or southwest Wisconsin for three days of golf. For us guys, it was all about playing golf and cards while drinking a lot of beer and partying.

Myrtle Beach golf with Dan Macumber, Mike Devine, Stan Reeg, and Dan Gisel.

After a few years of fishing trips to Wisconsin, I suggested to Dan Macumber that we didn't need to go fishing to play golf. We came up with the idea of organizing a spring golf trip each March to Biloxi, Mississippi. It was Dan Macumber, Dan Gisel, Mike Devine and myself. We had so much fun and made a lot of memories on those trips. We shared some great times. Mike and I treasure those memories. That's because life isn't always fair. Dan Macumber retired on April 1, 2002, after a 35-year career with Ralston Purina, which is now owned by Nestle. On April 30 he died in his sleep.

Dan did not make it to 60 years of age. His father lived to be 89, and his mother died at age 97. It makes you wonder, "How does that happen?" The shocking truth is, each of us, no matter what age we are, should live each day as if it could be our last and enjoy it for what it is.

I started out this New Year with a new four-word mantra: "Be in the moment." I have it written on a piece of paper taped on the bottom frame of my office computer. It is important to listen, be conscious of what is going on around you and enjoy the moments for what they are.

Dan Macumber's funeral Mass was held at St. Joseph's Church in DeWitt. When the funeral luncheon was over, I went over and talked to his widow Carol. I told her, "I'm going to start an annual charity golf tournament at Springbrook County Club in Dan's honor, and the profits will go to the benefit of Junior Achievement." I picked Junior Achievement because that's where Dan taught classes for grade school children the last several years before he died.

Each year, we gave most of the proceeds to our region's Junior Achievement, and we gave some to spina bifida because their daughter Jane had lost a child at birth to that disorder.

Mike Devine and I co-chaired the Macumber Memorial Golf Tournament for 13 continuous years along with Greg Barnes of Barnes Foodland and Pete Clausen of the Clausen Companies in Clinton. We raised a quarter of a million dollars for Junior Achievement in those 13 years. I believe Dan would not only be honored, but he would be pleased with the funds we have raised in his name for JA.

DeWitt has been a wonderful, perfect place to live and raise our children.

10th Anniversary
Dan Macumber Memorial
Junior Achievement Golf Tournament
2002-2012

"He was the answer to my prayers and together we had 4 great kids and wonderful grandchildren." -Carol

Carol and Dan Macumber. Almost $250,000 for Junior Achievement was raised in Dan's honor.

Chapter 8

A HARD WAY TO MAKE AN EASY LIVING

When Amway Calls, Ya Gotta Accept the Charges

In 1972, I was working at Farmall in the tractor assembly area when a man named John Holevoet befriended me. He told me about the Amway business and how it was a multilevel direct-selling business model. The idea was to sell some of the products direct to the consumer and, at the same time, to recruit others to do the same.

I was inspired by what I heard about many people from all types of backgrounds, businesses, and professions who had developed very successful Amway distributorships. I really didn't want to spend the rest of my life at Farmall. I was always looking for a way to get out of there. I thought Amway might be a pathway to becoming wealthy and getting out of Farmall.

When I first talked to Betty about it, she was quite leery of the whole proposition. After a few days of talking with John, he and his wife Cheryl, who was a really nice lady, drove about 70 miles from Galva, Illinois, to visit with us one evening. They were going to explain the story of Amway to us. Amway seemed like a good business because it had an excellent line of home care cleaning and personal hygiene products. Plus, they had the whole line of Nutrilite food supplements and vitamins, so it all made sense to me. My thought was, "They have good products. I can do this." I started out with a blaze of enthusiasm and excitement.

In the process of trying to recruit others, I talked to everyone I knew about the possibilities of creating a better life for themselves, their families, and their friends. When I look back on that experience, I realize that I had a missionary-type zeal for what I and others could accomplish. I had some success in recruiting friends and acquaintances in joining me in this great business. Within a few months, we had enough success that others began to recognize that Betty and I had potential in Amway.

At an early meeting that Betty and I attended, we were recognized for the level of success we had achieved and, of course, that inspired me to believe we could also become even more successful in the future! So, in addition to recruiting relatives, friends, and acquaintances, I started running blind ads in the *Clinton Herald*, a local newspaper, to recruit others to this great business.

At that time, when I wasn't working at Farmall, I was on the road recruiting distributors and helping other people recruit distributors. Once I started getting a few distributors in Clinton, Iowa, and Fulton, Illinois, I started holding weekly recruiting meetings at the Golden Corral in Clinton. The idea was that every one of our distributors could bring potential recruits to a group steak dinner, and I would do a presentation on how the Amway business worked. I explained to them how they, too, could realize their dreams by developing successful Amway businesses.

As we recruited more distributors throughout Iowa, Illinois, and Wisconsin, I would offer group recruiting presentations in public places and one-on-one presentations in people's homes. Because of our success, Vince and Alice Gaffey, who lived 40 miles away in Savanna, Illinois, continued to invite us to their Sunday Amway rallies, and Vince would ask Betty and me to get up in front of the audience and share our story on how we were creating our success.

In addition to having someone speak, Vince would generally introduce us to a new motivational book. That is when I first started reading inspirational, motivational books and a lot of autobiographies. That has really made a huge positive impact on how I think, how I conduct business, how I work with people, and how I relate to people.

As we started attending more Gaffey rallies, I was quite inspired by Vince. He always wore really nice clothes and suits and was always dressed to the nines. He had a great sense of humor. He enjoyed drinking and partying, which is something I was all game for. He was a great storyteller. He was always driving a new Cadillac or Lincoln. And with me being a car guy, I was impressed. His wife Alice was a stately, warm, and gracious hostess. We certainly had a lot of fun with those people, and thinking about it today brings back some pretty special memories.

The first book Vince shared with us was *Think and Grow Rich* by Napoleon Hill. Over the last 45 years, I've read that book 10 or 12 times. After that, I started reading more books, and I discovered many that I have read numerous times. Those books include *The Magic of Thinking Big, The Magic of Believing, The Power of Positive Thinking, Enthusiasm Makes a Difference, How I Raised Myself from Failure to Success, As a Man Thinketh, Your Greatest Power, Jonathan Livingston Seagull, Success Through a Positive Mental Attitude,* and *Creative Visualization.* Wayne Dyer has written more than 30 books, and I've read many of them numerous times. I also enjoy reading Joel Osteen's books, as I find them very inspirational.

The last 12 years at Farmall, I was a machinist. Many days at lunchtime, my coworkers would be eating at a metal picnic table in the middle of our department. While many of my co-workers were grumbling about how bad things were and all the negative things going on in the world, I would sit over by my machine and read books. I had set up a little workbench, and when I was on break or lunch hour, I would sit there reading inspirational books and stories while working on developing a positive attitude about life in general.

One of the guys I worked with was Glenn Granger. One day, after I had been in the department several years, he saw me reading those books. He said, "You know what? Someday, you're going to be very wealthy." He went on to say, "I believe that with all the books you're reading and the type of books you're reading, you can't help but become a millionaire." He said, "I'd appreciate it if you'd give me a call someday when you get to be worth $1 million."

Stan Reeg's "office" at Farmall. Note the inspirational book on top of the desk, 1982.

The Farmall plant closed a few years later, and I never saw Glenn again. A few years ago, when I was at a Farmall employee reunion with my brother Bill, we bumped into Dave, one of Glenn's friends. I tried the number Dave gave me a couple of times and never did get a response. When you get older, you appreciate seeing and visiting with the people you knew many years ago. Nevertheless, I wasn't calling Glenn to brag, but to tell him that his expectations—his beliefs in me—were fulfilled.

At one of the first Sunday meetings we attended at the Gaffey residence, Betty and I were recognized for generating $1,500 in sales in our Amway organization the previous month. That is quite a few bottles of soap and cleaners that we were selling for $1.90 a bottle! I was working more than 40 hours a week at Farmall, including overtime. Many nights and weekends, I was on the road and flying around to help other distributors build successful businesses. We had expanded into other states. I got my brother Don and his wife Linda in Colorado Springs involved. I flew out there a number of times to help them and their distributors recruit other people into the business.

Soon we were at the Gaffeys being recognized for reaching $4,000 a month in sales. At that time, my goal was to become a direct distributor, which is when you and your organization generates more than $7,500 a month in total sales volume for three consecutive months. With a lot of effort and enthusiasm, we soon reached that goal. We were recognized on a national level. The next time we went to the Amway national convention, it was at the convention center in downtown Grand Rapids, Michigan. That is the first time I met the founders, Rich DeVos and his wife Helen, plus Jay Van Andel and his wife Betty. I was impressed with how friendly and personable they all were.

Meanwhile, we had been holding weekly meetings in our basement, which we had finished out nicely. At that time, Betty was responsible for ordering the inventory and the products for our distributors. Distributors and customers would come by and get the products from us. Betty was doing a lot of weekly ordering. The merchandise would get shipped to our house, and then the distributors that we had recruited would come to our house and pick up the products they ordered for their customers and distributors.

The other big thing Betty did, which I didn't have the patience for, was a lot of counseling to help the distributors and guide them on how to be more successful. In those first years, we made a lot of 150-mile round-trips down to Galva, Illinois, to John and Cheryl's place to pick up inventory and attend meetings similar to what the Gaffeys were doing in Savanna. We made a lot of trips to Ada, Michigan, where Amway was headquartered. I also organized bus trips where we took many of our distributors with us to the annual conventions in Ada. Betty and I were recognized at one of these international conventions, as we had become a direct distributor. Of course, that's when we got to know Rich DeVos better.

Rich was a very personable individual. He would visit with you. His wife Helen was a wonderful lady as well. Rich was an exceptional public speaker, and he gave very inspiring talks. The success and the wealth that he and Jay Van Andel built amaze me. By 1980, they had purchased an island in the Caribbean called St. Peter Island. This was a nicely appointed resort, and some of the very top producers of Amway were invited there to spend time relaxing and enjoying the amenities. It was a resort island with staff, bartenders, housekeeping personnel, hospitality people, etc., there for your benefit.

In 1981, Rich DeVos was interested in owning an NBA team. He purchased his share of the Orlando Magic for $85 million dollars. Ironically his partner was Pat Williams who has been a friend of my co-author Rich Wolfe for many years.

Rich DeVos died in the summer of 2018, and his estimated net worth was in excess of $5.2 billion. His daughter-in-law Betsy DeVos is the United States Secretary of Education. People think just because they're wealthy, they don't care about the poor, but the DeVos family has donated more than $47 million dollars primarily to inner-city schools and educating minority students. Betsy was an excellent candidate to be the Secretary of Education. And how fitting, as Rich DeVos gave many talks on America and patriotism. He must have been quite pleased to see his daughter-in-law serving our country in that role.

Next we were Amway direct distributors and voting members because we had generated more than $7,500 a month for six months in a row. After becoming a direct distributor, the next goal was to help others accomplish that goal.

You've got to realize by now that Amway was pretty much my whole life other than working at Farmall and taking care of the family, which Betty did. By now, I was at the point where I didn't have time for anything outside of Amway. It was a total commitment.

We were helping others build their businesses when we hit the next recognition level, which was $15,000 per month in sales volume. For attaining that goal, Betty and I were recognized as Ruby Direct Distributors.

By this time, I was intent on achieving the next award level, which was becoming a Pearl Direct Distributor. This recognition meant you had three distributorships that you had sponsored in the business, and they each had to be doing $7,500 of sales volume in the month in the same month, not just $7,500 at different times.

Amway Recognition Levels: Red = $1,500, Blue = $4,000, Green = First month at $7,500.

Amway Award Levels: left to right, Direct Distributor, Ruby Direct Distributor, Pearl Direct Distributor with Voting Rights.

I was working day and night, weekends, and every spare minute I could at Amway. At the same time, the agriculture economy in our country was doing quite well. Farmall was developing a new helical gear drive transmission for their farm tractors. I was working as a machinist in the shop while finish gear grinding these new parts. That meant some weeks I was working seven days a week at my full-time job as well.

My primary role at the time was working with Farmall engineers to fine-tune the finished product—the gears—as they were in the development process. In order to finish these new helical-designed gears, Farmall purchased 18 innovative gear-grinding machines from Rheishauer, a company in Switzerland. Part of the purchase agreement was that Rheishauer would provide a skilled machinist/set-up man/service technician to Farmall for the next two years to train operators on how to set up the machines, run them, and service them, while generating high-quality precision gears.

The young man they sent here was an engineer and a precision machinist, Thomas Baumann. Being the outgoing person I had become by that time, I introduced myself to Tom and became his friend. More on Tom later.

By this time, Betty and I were giving talks around the country to other Amway organizations. Typically, there would be anywhere from 50 to 300 people in an arena, where we would address how we were successfully building our business. I was also giving motivational and inspirational talks. By now, I was really practicing what I had learned these past seven years or so from reading all of those motivational books and hearing other people's success stories.

I think the highlight of our speaking experience was when Amway flew Betty and me to Albuquerque to speak to a group of several hundred Amway distributors. That was a pretty cool experience compared to working in a manufacturing plant! A good speech should be like a pretty woman's skirt: long enough to cover the subject, short enough to create interest.

By now, we were approaching eight years in the Amway business. We had become Pearl Direct Distributors. I was working day and night. Initially when I got in the Amway business, my goal was to get to $100,000 annual income a year, and that's why I was working like a mad demon. I thought by now I would be successful and earning $100,000 a year, minimum. The past couple of years, we had made a little more than $30,000 with Amway, and I was making a bit more than $30,000 at Farmall by working a lot of overtime. I was spending most of the Amway money on gas, car expenses, hotel rooms, traveling, and promoting the business.

I taped our presentations as well as those of other successful Amway distributors. I bought a cassette tape duplicator. I placed the master tape in a slot, and the machine would duplicate two cassettes at a time. Betty was reproducing all those tapes, and we were selling them not only to our distributor organization, but to other Amway people who were interested in new ideas on how to successfully build their businesses.

By that time, Betty and I had built the organization to the point where we had distributors in 17 states. We had met a lot of great people, and we had more than 1,700 distributors in our organization. We felt it was a pretty successful organization, yet we were a long way from making $100,000 a year. It dawned on me that Amway was not the way for me to make that $100,000 a year that I was working so hard to accomplish. So, I decided to start looking around at other opportunities that I could execute on a part-time basis and perhaps make that $100,000 a year.

Little did I know at that time how all the experience I went through in the Amway business was preparing me for the most incredible opportunity in my life: getting into the investment business in 1985. I have always been a big proponent of the line, "When one door closes, another door opens." And it is always a better door if you are a positive thinker.

Chapter 9

FROM NUTS AND BOLTS TO PUTTS AND QUOTES

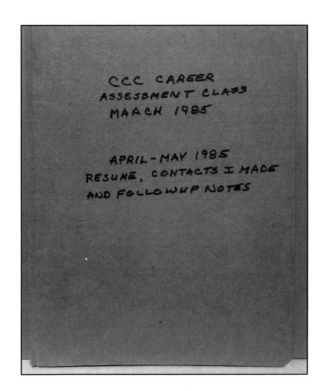

Down at the Corner of What and If

Once the announcement to close the Farmall plant was made in 1985, it led to disaster in the lives of many former employees. Many of the employees started drinking alcohol heavily; or maybe were to begin with, but they became alcoholics. A lot of people got divorced. They just could not deal with the adversity. I was fortunate that I went through the Job Training Program Act program through Clinton Community College and figured out what I was naturally, intuitively, most ideally suited for as a career. Many of the others, in addition to having those issues, were forced to move to other plants around the country, including some in Indiana and Ohio. The other International Harvester companies that were acquired by J. I. Case, would remain open; people would retire, and the company would need more employees if they increased production. Many of the employees I worked with moved to those plants, but I decided my goal was to never, ever work in a factory again in my life!

In fact, when I first started in the investment business (and even many years thereafter), what really motivated me if I had a bad month were the nightmares—that I was back at that factory, running those machines. It was that insecurity I experienced the first 20 years I was in the investment business. That fear is part of what motivated me to do better, be bigger, and be more successful. I just did not want to deal with failure, and I never wanted to go back to one of those factories. That is part of the blessing that has motivated me to become one of the top producers in our industry and in my company.

By the time the Farmall plant closing was announced, Dan Macumber had become a very good friend of mine. Dan knew many of the personnel managers in the area, as he had been a personnel manager for Ralston Purina for many years. When I was finally laid off for the last time in 1985, he said, "Stan, I'm going to help you get a job." He introduced me to other job opportunities in the Quad Cities. One of them was DuPont in Clinton. The other was at Alcoa in Bettendorf. Actually, Alcoa interviewed me a couple of times after reviewing my resume and I was thinking they would hire me. They had me take a physical exam and then, when a job opening came up, if it was a match to my skill set, they would call me, and I would be ready to go to work the next day.

Once I got over the shock of Farmall announcing the closing of the plant, I decided I had better reassess and evaluate what my employment possibilities might be. Before that shocking announcement, I was on the "30 years and out" plan, which was what many of my coworkers were on as well. That was, once you had 30 years in seniority, no matter what age you were, you could retire and get a full pension. When the plant closed, I had 21-years total pension time credit between the two International Harvester plants (in East Moline and Farmall Works in Rock Island). I was only 38 years old, as I had started in the factory at East Moline when I was 17 years old.

I started to take inventory of my skills and abilities. There weren't many, as I never completed my college education. I had attended Black Hawk Community College part-time, and I had earned 24 college credit hours. At the time, there was massive unemployment in the agriculture manufacturing sector of the U.S. economy. At the time I was pretty apprehensive and concerned about how I was going to provide for my family. The United States government started offering classes through the Job Training Program Act at the local community colleges in eastern Iowa.

Several weeks after I became unemployed, I attended a week-long career and assessment evaluation class free of charge at Clinton Community College. There, I did numerous dexterity, aptitude, and attitude exercises. On Friday noon, you added up each of the scores linearly, and you looked in a six-inch thick book for your score. When I found that number, the result was that I was most ideally suited to be a securities analyst or securities broker. That was an easy decision for me to make because I wasn't going to be an analyst. This was quite surprising to me because when I was a young child, I didn't even know what a stockbroker was! And now I was going to become one.

In early 2018, I met Ann Eisenman, the executive director of Clinton Community College Foundation. I had sponsored the "Dinner with Marilyn Monroe" event at the Figge Art Museum in Davenport that evening. Roger Hill from DeWitt Bank and Trust had informed her of the book I was writing and relayed to her that all the proceeds from my book were going to benefit of the Paul B. Sharar Foundation. This is because of my gratitude to Clinton Community College for holding that vocational planning class in March 1985. Following that exercise, I pursued a career in the financial services industry and have earned millions of dollars for my clients.

At that time, Betty and I were doing our banking with DeWitt Bank and Trust, and Jon Billhorn was the president of the Bank. On the following Monday morning I stopped by the bank and told him about the previous week's experience and that I was looking for his opinion. His comment was, "I believe you would make a good securities broker," and he asked if I knew his friend, Gordy Berst. I didn't know Gordy, so Jon offered to introduce me to him. Gordy had been in the securities business for more than 30 years by that time. He worked with Jack Beyer and Co. in Davenport. Gordy lived in DeWitt at Springbrook Country Club and was quite successful.

Later that week, Gordy stopped by the house on his way home from his office to critique my resume. The most important suggestion he made was for me to state that my near-term goal was to make $100,000 a year. That was music to my ears, as that had been my goal all the years I had been in Amway. The past 14 years, that had been my goal.

He told me I should go to Merrill Lynch, as they would most likely hire and train me. After a couple of years of building up my clientele and becoming successful, I could go to work with Gordy.

The following week, I started dropping off my resumes at several investment firms, including A.G. Edwards, Dain Bosworth, Blunt, Ellis, & Loewi, Dean Witter, Robert Baird, E. F. Hutton, and last of all, Merrill Lynch, Pierce, Fenner & Smith. I wanted to build my business at Merrill because they were a well-known investment firm and they had just moved into a new brick office complex building.

The previous Sunday at St. Joe's Church, I bumped into Dean and Bev Frey, who were former Amway distributors of ours. I asked Bev what her sister Diane was doing in Minneapolis. She told me that Diane recently started at Merrill Lynch as an investment advisor. I said, "What kind of pay did she start out with?" Bev said, "Well, I don't know what the bonus system was, but she started out with a guaranteed $25,000 the first year as a base, plus commissions." I thought to myself, "I could survive on that income, at least in the beginning."

It seemed to me that the stars were lining up, and I was feeling pretty optimistic. Since I had not interviewed for a job in more than 20 years, I thought it best to arrange interviews at different investment firms so that when I interviewed at Merrill, I would be experienced at interviewing. When I finally visited the Merrill Lynch office, the branch manager's assistant reviewed my resume. She asked me if I would be willing to take three five-minute tests to determine if I might be a good candidate for Merrill Lynch's training program. She told me that the manager would not even visit with me unless I scored well on those tests.

One was a vocabulary test, one was a math test, and the third was a spelling test. After she scored and reviewed my test results, she said, "I'm sure the manager will want to talk to you." That same day, I received a call from Jack Stengel, who was the branch manager at Dain Bosworth in downtown Davenport. He was responding to the resume I had dropped off the previous week.

After a number of interviews and other testing, I was offered jobs at both Dain Bosworth and Merrill Lynch, and now I had a tough decision to make. I knew if I was calling a prospective client from Merrill Lynch, the prospect would know why I was calling. I had never heard of Dain Bosworth before! The only reason I left a resume at the office was because the outdoor sign on the corner of the building noted they were members of the New York Stock Exchange.

After a few weeks of going back and forth between the two, I ended up choosing Dain Bosworth for two reasons. First, Dain Bosworth had the best training program in America for investment advisors. Second, Merrill Lynch had suggested I come in some morning and just sit in individually with some of the financial advisors and monitor some of their conversations to get a feel for how they conducted business. I still have the notes and names of the five different financial advisors (FAs) that I visited with that morning. One of them was on the phone talking to a client when I walked into his office and sat down as the manager had instructed me to do. When the broker hung up the phone, he acted quite suspicious about why I was monitoring him in spite of the fact that I told him what the manager had instructed me to do. He really didn't want to visit with me, either. It was a very uncomfortable situation for me, so I finally walked out of his office and into another FA's office. This was a red flag for me. Even today when I think about the situation, it makes me wonder why he felt so insecure about me being in his office. My guess is that he may have been using some unethical practices and thought perhaps I was a security investigator for the firm.

I left the Merrill Lynch office thinking it would not be a friendly, helpful environment in which I could build my business. I called Jack Stengel down at Dain Bosworth and asked him if I could come down to visit with him again. He told me I could, but I am sure by this time he was wishing I had made a decision. Luckily, Jack was a patient person. I drove downtown to the Dain office and told Jack my dilemma. He told me, "Why don't I have you visit with my assistant branch manager

Bob Fowler, who has been in the investment business for over 30 years?"

Bob was a consummate salesman, and he was a very passionate individual, especially about the investment business. He and I were having a good visit, and finally I told him my dilemma. I said, "Why should I go to work with you guys when I can go to work at Merrill Lynch?" He said, "Because you've got to!" and he just started laughing. He didn't say anything else. Of course, I knew by then in sales that the first person who speaks loses. He did not say a word, and I chuckled and said, "Well, I guess I'm going to work at Dain Bosworth." I made my decision in that moment.

After wrapping up our visit, Jack informed me I would start my career on May 15, 1985, at their office in downtown Davenport. I have thanked Jack many times over the years for the opportunity he gave me, but I never will be able to thank him enough! Now when I look back on my decision, I know I made the correct one for me. Dain had a great mentoring program that really helped me build a successful business.

Part of the big deal about going to work with Dain was they had a great training program, but I was going to have to live in Minneapolis for the four summer months of 1985. There were 19 of us in my class, and they were from Denver, Boulder, Seattle, Lincoln (Nebraska), Kansas City, Las Vegas, Duluth, and the Minneapolis and St. Paul areas. The first day I arrived in the Davenport office, Dain Bosworth's training department had already sent me the list of everyone who would participate in that four-month training program. They also sent a list of potential accommodations. The suggestions were to stay at a hotel or rent a condominium. I decided I would lease a three-bedroom condominium for those four months.

There was a Roger Tabor from Las Vegas on the list of trainees. As I didn't know anyone from Las Vegas, I called and asked him to join me in leasing the loft condo on the Mississippi

River in the old warehouse district of downtown Minneapolis. He agreed and told me he was looking forward to meeting me and spending the summer with me in Minneapolis.

I also called Mike Gegen from Denver, and he agreed to join Roger and myself in the condominium arrangement. Interestingly enough, against all odds, the three of us have become very successful and are still in the investment business.

We spent the next four months together. We would walk from our condominium across the Mississippi River over to the Dain Bosworth Tower in downtown Minneapolis. We completed all of our classwork, exams, and the Series Seven Exam, which was a seven-hour test at that time. Then we had to prepare a business plan for our first year of production for when we arrived back in our respective branches. Following that, we were each interviewed individually by the president of retail sales at Dain Bosworth.

As I prepared my business plan, I decided, "Getting into this business and getting hired is my opportunity. It's just a matter of how big a goal I have, how much energy I am willing to put forth, how many hours I am willing to work, and how many contacts I am willing to make." I looked at this as my gold mine, and it was my opportunity of a lifetime. One of the concepts I learned in my Amway days was to develop a plan and work the plan.

The goal I established for my first year was to generate a total commission of $100,000 in fees and commissions for the firm. When the president of retail sales, Ron Tschetter, interviewed me and reviewed my business plan, he said, "You know, we don't have many rookies do $100,000 in their first year." My immediate response was, "Maybe that is because you don't expect them to." The first year I did more than $110,000 in gross commissions, and I generated all of my business as a result of cold calling from two different lists that I had purchased from Dun and Bradstreet when I was in Minneapolis. The one list was couples that were over the age of 50 and earning in excess of $50,000 a year. The other list was officers of closely held businesses and publicly traded companies. Those leads were comprised of presidents, vice presidents, treasurers, secretaries, and other high-level executives. The lists I had purchased contained individuals who were all within fifty miles of the Davenport office. I primarily had a list of people in the Quad Cities, Clinton and Muscatine (Iowa), and Morrison, Fulton, and Galesburg (Illinois). I then asked the office receptionist to screen my prospective client lists so I wouldn't be calling existing Dain Bosworth clients.

Before I went to Minneapolis for the four months of training, I was in the Davenport branch for two weeks. I was required to develop a list of at least 1,000 prospective clients I would use as contacts when I arrived back in the branch after my training. The resources I used to come up with those names, addresses, and phone numbers were the Polk directory and the Yellow Pages of the local Quad City phone book and the same for each of those other communities.

Interestingly enough, the first clients who had more than $1 million worth of investments with me were Bill and Shirley Meredith of Bettendorf, Iowa. They came from a cold call I made from the initial list I compiled from the Polk directory. I had called Bill with the idea of possibly investing in an AAA-rated tax-free municipal bond. He said it sounded interesting, but didn't make any commitment. I called him several more times after that. After four or five conversations with Bill, I asked if I could come out and visit with him and Shirley at their house on a Friday afternoon. He graciously accepted, and we scheduled the time.

Bill was a retired human resources director from John Deere Plow Planter Works in Moline. I told him that my dad was retired from John Deere Dubuque Tractor Works after 30 years of employment. I also told him that I worked for a couple of months at Deere Planter back in 1970 when I was laid off from

Farmall. He and Shirley were very warm and open with me. He liked the tax-free idea I initially presented to him on the phone and asked what other ideas I had. The result was that after I presented some of my other ideas to him, he wrote a $70,000 check out to Dain Bosworth for me to invest. Boy, was I on cloud nine!

At this point in my career, I had only been in the business a few months, and I had never had a new client invest $50,000 or more on their initial investment with me. At that time, Jim Murphy was the top producer in our office, and I admired his success. He became a mentor of mine. Many days, he was getting all kinds of $50,000+ orders. I thought, "Man, if only someday I could do that!"

As I was cold calling, I realized from the beginning that it was going to be a tough uphill battle. It would be like climbing a mountain, but I also realized that it was a numbers game. I knew that the more contacts I made and the more failure I had, the more success I would later have.

When I was making some of these contacts and started getting some interest from prospective clients, or when they would ask me questions that I didn't know the answer to, I would ask Bob Fowler the same question. Bob was a consummate sales- man, and he was always full of ideas. The other person who was invaluable to me was Gary Aronson. I can't thank him today because he has passed, but every time I saw him after I left Dain Bosworth, I always thanked Gary for all he did to help me when I first started in the business.

Gary was a great guy. He came into the business a few years before I did. Previously, he was a school teacher, and after that, he sold industrial equipment for a period of time. Having been a teacher, he was very patient and a positive influence on me. When I had questions, Gary would drop everything he was doing to assist me. He was incredibly nice to me, and I will never forget it. Gary and Bob Fowler were of major assistance to me, as they always had good ideas and responses to questions for which I did not have answers.

Dan Macumber, my DeWitt friend, was a big cheerleader and supporter of my decision. Dan had said, "Stan, I'm not going to buy stock from you. If I could buy stock in YOU, that would be what I would do. I know you will be successful!" In the early days in the investment business, that was a pretty important remark because it helped build my confidence and made me think, "Hey, maybe I can be successful in this business."

I was not naïve. I realized that for me to succeed in the investment business, it would be a numbers game: I didn't know anyone with money. I knew that if I wanted to be successful, I needed to track my activities. Initially, I kept track of every call I made, the number of solid contacts I had, the number of new accounts I opened each day and week, the amount of new assets I gathered, and the gross revenue that was generated from those activities. I also kept track of how many hours per week I was working. I have to tell you, that first day when I landed back in the branch and was going to start making those cold calls, it was pretty frightening. In fact, I felt a little nauseated and apprehensive, but I gathered my wits, picked up one of those Dun and Bradstreet leads and dialed. Inside, I was hoping they wouldn't answer, but I knew sooner or later I had to face the devil. I just gave myself a little "pep talk" before each call and methodically made those calls. The first three weeks, I opened five new account relationships and generated $1,518 of gross commissions.

My initial goal was to make 125 qualified contacts per week, and these weren't dials or just phone numbers. These were solid contacts where if I talked to somebody in the household and they were not the decision maker for the family's investments, I did not count them. My goal was to make 25 solid contacts a day, five days a week. I kept track of all the statistics and recorded them in a little red spiral 25-cent notebook each week. Talk about return on investment!

Most weeks, I called during regular business hours, from 9 a.m. until 5 p.m. I would call businesspeople and retirees at different times during the day. On Tuesday and Thursday evenings, I generally worked or called until 9 p.m. If I didn't make my 125 contacts for the week, I would go to the office Saturday morning to complete them.

Notebooks that Stan Reeg tracked important weekly stats for his first four years in the business.

I will never forget one Saturday as I was making call No. 122 for the week. I had cold called Terry O'Connell with the Franklin U.S. Government Securities Mutual Fund. After I made my presentation, he said, "I'll take $20,000." I was quite taken back and once I gathered my wits, I asked him for all his personal information in order to open an account the following Monday. The one thing it confirmed to me is that I could be successful using cold-calling as a method of obtaining clients. That was very early in my career, and in the next 30 years, I never had anyone make an investment on the first call again.

Once I got the hang of cold calling effectively, my goal was not to sell the prospect anything. My goal was to get a face-to-face appointment with the prospect and his/her spouse. To be a success at cold-calling, you had to have a lot of fortitude because people would swear at you. People would hang up on you. People would be very disrespectful. But, some people were kind and very nice to you. You've got to realize the environment in which I was working: I was in a bullpen where there were 15 other FAs sitting in little cubicles, like many of the secretaries in corporate offices did in those days. They were fabric-covered cubicles that stood about 4-feet tall around the perimeter and were maybe six-foot square spaces.

I felt bad for the advisors who were working with me because when I was making cold calls, I talked loudly—especially when I was nervous, which was most of the time. So everyone in the office could hear my pitch and my responses to potential clients' questions.

There were many a day I went home feeling beat up and depressed. When I had days like that, I would just go home, strip off my suit, go directly to bed and sleep for maybe 12 hours. The next morning, I would get up, put my suit on and be the first one in the office, and I would be back on that phone! I was determined to be successful and was willing to work until hell froze over and then to work on ice if I had to!

Bob Fowler was the assistant branch manager, and he was always reassuring me that with the effort he had seen me putting forth, I would not be denied success. In fact, he told me that if I continued doing what I was doing for the next five years, I would be able to live the remainder of my life in a way that most people would never be able to experience. Plus, he said, I would be very successful. That was an inspirational message to me.

During my Amway days, I read a lot of motivational and inspirational books. I decided I needed to reward myself for the success I had with my cold calling effort. In the beginning, whenever I had a good month, I would reward myself by buying a new tie. I would go to a fine men's clothing store called the Gentry Shop, which was just down the block from our office in downtown Davenport.

What you have to realize is that at that time, I had only a couple of suits. I wore a suit to the office every day. It's pretty hard to rotate your wardrobe when you have only two suits. After buying a number of ties, I started buying a nice suit if I had a record month. I figured I got beat up enough cold calling that I needed to reward myself. I don't do that these days. Instead, when I have a great month, I give more money to charity. I just need to make sure I am contributing to causes in which I believe.

In my early career days, I asked my oldest son Todd to drive into Clinton, Iowa, to the local Mercedes dealership and request the latest Mercedes-Benz sales brochure. I ended up cutting out a three-by-five-inch picture of a new dark blue 300 E Mercedes-Benz. Before getting into the investment business, I never earned more than $30,000 per year. After I cut that picture out, I took it to my office and posted it on the fabric wall behind my phone. At that time, two of the financial advisors in our office were driving leased 318 BMWs, but I wanted a car that was more sophisticated and made a statement. So I chose a Mercedes-Benz. I had a desk and was sharing a Quotron machine with Bob Fowler, who was in the adjoining cubicle.

Cold calling was quite an experience. When people would hang up on me, I would just gut it out—pick up the phone and dial another prospect. I kept seeing that Mercedes-Benz photo and saying, "I'm going to buy one of those cars one of these days, and I am going to pay cash for it."

That was in the fall of 1985. In 1986, there was a retired couple, Bob and Jane Morey, who were rather affluent and had become clients of mine. One day shortly after I hung the Mercedes-Benz picture up on my cubicle wall, they were meeting with me, and Jane said, "What is that picture there behind your phone?" I told her, "Well, once I meet my production goal, I am going to buy that new Mercedes-Benz." Every time they came into the office after that, she would always ask me, "How are you coming on getting that Mercedes-Benz?" Fortunately, they lived long enough to see me reach my goal and enjoy that new Mercedes-Benz. What I learned from that experience is that your clients want to see you succeed and enjoy sharing in your success with you. As an investor, the reality is that you naturally want to work with an advisor who is successful.

First Mercedes, E-300, 1989

I learned various techniques on how to have more success on my cold calls. One of them was before I started dialing, I would consciously put a smile on my face. I still do it today because I really believe that the person on the other end of the telephone line can tell you've got a smile on your face. It makes people feel more relaxed and open. I also realized that if I wanted to be successful, I needed to work with wealthy people. At that time, my use of the English language was pretty bad. So when I got on the phone, I would consciously monitor how I was talking to people and the words I was using.

After about 10 months of working with all of these three-by-five Dun and Bradstreet lead cards, I had them spread all over my desk and on the floor. I realized I needed to get a more efficient system in place. When I would call someone who was a solid contact, I'd write a note on the card. I would record what information I had sent them and a callback date. I had learned by that time that before you would ever get somebody to come in and see you or before they would invest with you, you had to have about five conversations or contacts with them. I spent hours at the end of each business day sending notes, business cards and brochures about Dain Bosworth or various types of investments to everyone I talked to that day. If they had any positive tone in their response to my call, I would send them something with my business card included, as that was my excuse to be able to call them back.

Actual Dun and Bradstreet Lead Card

By this time, I was totally disorganized. There were no yellow sticky notes in those days, but I had these D&B file cards covered in handwritten notes. The potential clients I never reached, I would note when I last tried to contact them. In mid-1986, I decided I needed to purchase my own computer in order to load and update all my contacts and the content of my conversations, plus the materials I mailed to each of the prospects and when my next call date was to be.

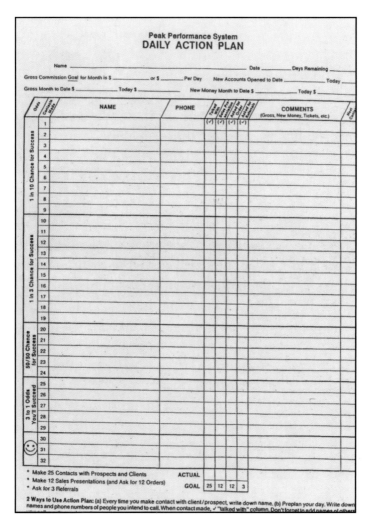

Phil Broyle's Daily Action Plan

The other tool I started using at that time was a green daily action plan that had 32 lines on it for names of people I talked to that day. I had attended a Phil Broyles seminar in Minneapolis, and that is what he recommended. He felt most advisors believed they were making a lot of calls, but the only way to determine that was to track the calls. Here we are 30 years later, and I still use that green call sheet!

In all the years I've been in this business, I've noticed that most advisors are rather cheap and never want to spend any of their own money on building their practice. They always feel that the firm owes them that, but my attitude was if it will help me be a better advisor for my clients, it's just a cost of doing business. When you invest in your business, you expect to get a return, and that was my primary thought on why the computer was going to make me more efficient. It also was going to make me more effective with my follow-up on the relationships I was developing. I have notes in my computer on all the conversations I've had with every client since those days.

I knew the odds of success in my new industry were not good. When we were in our training class in Minneapolis, our instructor told us, "In the first year, 25 percent of you won't make the cut, and after five years, only 25 percent of you will still be in the business." Knowing that I had never obtained a college degree, I realized this was my chance to not only succeed, but to become wealthy. I truly did look at the investment business as my path to success or, in another sense, my goldmine. You keep working through your list of prospects and keep talking to them. It's just like turning over stones in a goldmine—sooner or later, you are going to find some gold!

I knew it was a numbers game and what the odds were. I was very persistent and hell-bent on succeeding. Furthermore, I did not give myself an out. I told myself early on, "This is one thing I will be successful at, and I will do everything within my power to succeed!" There were no acceptable excuses. I made the calls—I had to do it! In those days, I did not know anyone of significant net worth. None of my family members had any wealth in those days. None of my friends or coworkers had wealth, so I had no choice but to cold call, and that I did.

Basically, no excuses for me to fail were acceptable! In my second year, I continued to do cold calling. Then I started working to obtain referrals. In my second year, I did $161,490 of gross production for the firm. One of my goals was to open three new accounts each week, which I pretty much did each of my first four years in the business. I generally opened anywhere from 150 to 250 new client accounts in each of my first four years in the business.

I also kept track of how many dollars of cash and/or assets I was bringing in and how much revenue I was generating each week and month. I tracked how many new accounts I was opening and the number of hours I was working. Thirty years later, I still have that little three-by-five-inch spiral notebook where I tracked and recorded all my statistics for the first four years.

Numbers tell the story.

It is a contact business!

My strategy and efforts yielded exceptional results. Out of the 19 members of my class from larger-populated cities in the United States, I was the No. 1 producer three of the first four years. In 1989, I did more than $250,000 of production, and that is the first year I exceeded $100,000 in W-2 income, which was my initial goal when I started in this business.

In the fall of 1986, I was one year in the business at Dain Bosworth when one of the advisors was terminated for lack of generating new clients and new business. One evening after he was let go, I was looking for a Rolodex in his credenza and found a whole batch of Dun & Bradstreet cards similar to the leads I had purchased the year before. It was a list of business owners and executive-level employees of public and privately held companies in northwestern Illinois. Give me a lick on that lollipop!

I could see the departed broker's handwritten notes and dates of when he talked to some of them. As I reviewed the leads, I threw away many of the cards. One of the cards listed Anton Zueger as the president of Avanti Foods in Walnut, Illinois, 60 miles away. I thought the name sounded German or Swiss, so a few days later I called Tony and had a nice visit with him. He told me he was in the cheese business and that all of his advisors were Swiss. That included his CPA, his investment advisors, and his attorney.

He told me that I sounded like a nice young man and some day when I got over his way, I should stop and see him. A few weeks later, I called to tell him I would be in Walnut around 10 a.m. on Wednesday of the next week. He suggested he would be available. On Wednesday, I drove the hour over to Walnut and met him at the cheese factory headquarters. I had a great visit with him, but he told me he was happy with his current financial advisors. He suggested that I stay in touch with him. So, about once a quarter, I would call Tony and visit with him.

When the 1987 stock market crash hit, Tony's Swiss advisor decided to move back to Switzerland. The next time I called Tony, he told me, "You are my advisor now!" I scheduled an appointment to visit him at his business and get better acquainted on a personal and financial level. Being the astute businessman he was, he had other investment accounts spread around the country.

He and his wife Josy, were Swiss immigrants who came to the United States in the early 1950s. He was a cheesemaker by trade and by now had developed a very successful cheesemaking company. He also had his own pizza manufacturing company plus a retail shop in town where he sold many different types of cheese, cheese curds, sausage, Swiss confectionaries, and Swiss chocolates. He and Josy were wonderful people, and we all had a very profitable relationship. As I said, he was an astute businessman, and he tracked portfolio performance on a daily basis. Back in those days, he and I started out picking high-quality blue-chip stocks of companies when they were out of favor and their stock prices were down.

In the late 1980s and early 1990s, there were a number of years when we had in excess of 30% annualized gains on Tony and Josy's portfolio. Because of Tony's astute business acumen and success, some of his closest friends ended up becoming clients of mine. He and Josy have long since passed away, but all three of their children and some of their grandchildren are now clients of mine. I have been very blessed because as I have developed my business, the focus has always been on the relationships with the client and their family, not on how much money I can make. It is the old adage—if you just take care of others, you will be taken care of.

In the late 1980s, a couple in suburban Chicago, Rudy and Martha, were some of Tony and Josy Zueger's closest friends. One afternoon, I received a phone call from Rudy, and he told me Tony had suggested that he call me, as he was not happy with his financial advisor in Chicago. Tony had told him that of all the financial advisors he ever worked with, "Stan was the best." I told Rudy I could come over to Winnetka on Saturday morning just to have a get-acquainted visit.

Our oldest son Todd was home from college on a holiday break. That Saturday, he rode to Chicago with me since it was about a three-hour drive each way. Once we concluded our meeting, the family decided they were going to transfer all their investment accounts to me.

Over the years, not only have Rudy and Martha been wonderful clients, but they have become like family to me. Years before I met them, they had made a couple of investments in New Glarus, Wisconsin, which is like a Swiss village. When you go there, one of the attractions is the New Glarus Brewery, which features a renowned beer called "Spotted Cow." When the founders of the brewery first started the business, they were not well financed. Rudy and Martha owned a commercial building in downtown New Glarus that they rented to the family. Since they could not afford to pay rent with cash, they gave Rudy and Martha shares of their company stock instead.

Over about a 20-year period, the brewery continued to grow and have a lot of success. The owners started paying substantial dividends on the stock. A few years ago, the family who owns New Glarus Brewery decided they wanted to buy back all the outstanding shares of stock. Rudy and Martha called me all excited, as they were going to be receiving a large sum of money.

Since this was newfound wealth that they were not expecting, I suggested they, their three sons, and I should convene a legacy and family estate planning meeting with their estate attorney in downtown Chicago. As a result, they did some serious gifting to the three boys, and they all started relationships with me. I am looking forward to being of value to the boys, their spouses, and their children in the years ahead. We have already funded 529 Plans and UTMA accounts for the grandchildren over the years. The 529 Plans are tax-advantaged accounts specifically designed to accumulate funds for advanced or higher education. All the investments in 529 Plans are required to be mutual funds. Previous to the origination of 529 Plans, I funded Uniform Trust for Minors Accounts (UTMAs). They are also tax-efficient plans than can be used for any purpose, but when liquidated, the beneficiary will have income tax consequences. When the child becomes 21 years of age those UTMA assets become theirs, whereas the person who owns and contributed the funds to the 529 Plan controls the account no matter what age the beneficiary has attained.

This is the typical client for us, as we are all about the relationship. We are monitoring the tax advice and estate planning guidance our clients are utilizing. In most cases, we know our clients' situations better and in more depth than any of their other professional advisors. We view ourselves as the financial quarterback to assisting them in having the best tax, estate and legacy planning that is most pertinent their personal situations. People who don't plan for retirement often find out later they can't afford to keep up with the payments on the American Dream.

As for Rudy and Martha, they both immigrated to Chicago from Switzerland when they were young adults. He worked for a printing company while Martha worked at the Saks Fifth Avenue in downtown Chicago. Later, Rudy decided to start his own printing company and became quite successful. He sold it after 30 years of success to Wicklander Press, which was a publicly traded company. That is about the time Tony introduced me to Rudy and Martha.

Another story about Tony Zueger is many years later when I attended his funeral in Walnut, the family held a luncheon following the Mass. His daughter, Doris, seated me next to her lifelong friend Ann. We had a delightful visit in spite of the occasion. She asked me a lot of questions about investing. She then revealed to me that her parents had been using an A.G. Edward's advisor in a northwest Chicago suburb, and she was not impressed with the lack of communication with her now that she had power of attorney for her mother's accounts. Ann has her own law practice, and her husband Tom has his own specialized dental practice in Bourbonnais, Illinois, in which he works only with private pay patients. They are the nicest people! Needless to say, we have developed a great relationship.

The most recent story about Tony involves a young couple from Walnut who contacted me about possibly using my services. They came over to Davenport to get acquainted and see if I might be of value to them. The prospective client's mother worked for Tony for more than 35 years, so it would be pretty hard to say no to them and their financial planning needs.

Another lead I found in the credenza was Don and Marsha Pedersen, who had made one investment with the departed broker in 1985. It was a Dain Bosworth real estate limited partnership. Since Don was a successful business owner, I thought he might be interested in owning another Dain real estate partnership. As it ended up, the first investment they did with me was Dain 86 real estate partnership. From that point on, I worked on developing a trusting relationship with Don over several years. It seems that with his engineering background, he was a bit suspect of a financial advisor's motives when recommending investments to him as a client.

Over the years, not only have he and his family become trusting clients, but they have become very successful investors as well. Marsha actually did a testimonial on the back cover of one of my audio books in 1995. After Marsha's parents retired and moved to Iowa, I worked with them on their investment portfolio as well. Don and Marsha have referred other family members to me over the years, and we have become good friends in the process.

> "Our business is one of 'trust'."

Many of my clients are respected, successful business leaders in their communities, and other people will follow their lead on whom to use as a professional advisor. Our business is one of "trust." By the time a client comes to work with us, they are generally entrusting us with their lifetime accumulation of wealth, and we don't take that responsibility lightly.

March 1989 is when I had earned enough income to pay cash for my first Mercedes-Benz. It was not a brand new car, but it was a 1987 300 E Mercedes-Benz with a black exterior and black interior. It was exciting as it was the realization of a goal set four years previously.

Many times when you achieve big goals like that, a person has a tendency to sit on their laurels. You plateau because you are comfortable at that level of success. It is really easy to do, and it happens to many talented people in our industry. Guess what you do next? You have to establish larger goals, change how you are doing things, and most of all get outside your comfort zone again!

◇ ◇ ◇

The next story is about Dr. Robert Donnelly and his family. When I first started in the Investment Business, I was very involved with the Knights of Columbus, and I generally tended to go to the monthly meetings that they held at the KC Hall. One of the longtime members of the Knights of Columbus was Cal Donnelly and his wife Marge, who attended many KC functions. Cal was a 'good ole boy' that I really liked. He was a truck driver and I believe he belonged to the Teamsters Union. He is someone that probably never earned over thirty thousand dollars a year on his primary job. After I'd been in the Business a while, one Monday evening after a KC meeting, Cal said to me, "You need to call my son. He's a doctor." I said, "Yeah, yeah, I'll call him."

Bob and I agreed to meet over lunch on a specific day. His wife Lynn didn't come with him, as he came directly from the clinic. Bob is associated with Medical Associates Clinic in Clinton, Iowa. Nevertheless, we had a really nice lunch, with a lot of good conversation. Bob was impressed with how I managed my investment practice and how I worked with clients. He told me he would give serious consideration to transferring his assets and doing his retirement plan investing with me.

What happened next is quite interesting and something I will never forget. Since I arrived early at Clinton Country Club, I was in the first parking spot for guests at the Club. So, when we came walking out of the Country Club, and as we approached my car I stopped. He said to me, "Is this your car?" I said, "Yes, it is my car." He responded, "Oh, man, I was always hoping that my Investment Advisor would be driving a Mercedes-Benz."

I never asked him why he made that comment, but I believe there were two reasons. One is that he came from a family that did not have a lot of money, and he had to work his way through medical school, and paid for much of his medical schooling on his own. The other issue was being the bright individual Bob is, he figured that if his Advisor was driving a Mercedes-Benz, he was successful, and he must know something about how to help people become successful investors.

We have worked together over the years to develop him a plan so that at the time he turns sixty two years of age, he would be in a financial position to be able to retire. Much like many of my other clients, Bob and Lynn, and their family are really nice people and I enjoy working with the family as a whole.

Hopefully, one of these days, he will feel like he is in a position to retire. Financially he is there, but the cost of family health care insurance coverage is such a huge unknown liability in our Country today, it's hard for people to retire. Many clients would like to retire, but in most cases, they don't retire until age 65, because the future cost of health care insurance, is so uncertain. At least at age sixty-five they can go on Medicare and Medicare supplement which is within most people's budget. If you are retiring before age sixty five, you don't know what your health care plans will cost. In some cases, it's as much as $1,900 a month or more for a family plan.

Bob is one of those people that has other interests he would consider pursuing if he knew the number that his maximum Family Medical Care Insurance costs would be capped.

◇◇◇

At Dain Bosworth, we received monthly industry publications with stories of how other advisors had built successful practices. One story I was particularly impressed with was the "Cold Call Cowboy." His name was Stephen W. Anderson, and he had written a 40-page typewritten booklet that was titled

"How to Become a Million-Dollar Producer." In those days, being a million-dollar producer made you a "star" at the firm, and that is what I intended to become.

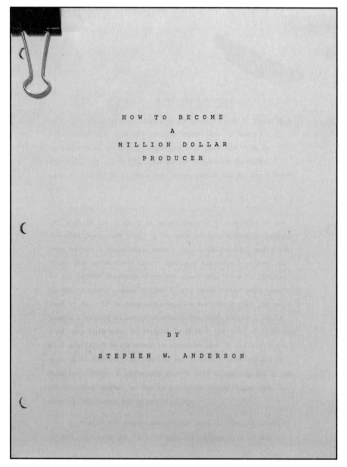

HOW TO BECOME
A
MILLION DOLLAR
PRODUCER

BY

STEPHEN W. ANDERSON

One of the "Cold Call Cowboy's" first publications

Steve was located in Palm Springs, California, and that's where he built a very successful investment business by cold calling. One of the first award trips we earned with Dain Bosworth was in 1990, to Palm Desert, California. I knew that Steve's headquarters were in Palm Springs, so I made a point of going to his office and having a personal consultation with him. We discussed many business-building ideas, and the one I found most interesting was the audio business card he had developed.

First Audio Business Card

His audio book was 6 x 9 inches and 5/8 of an inch-thick plastic container that looked like a book. It was about the size of a small storybook. When I developed mine, there was a picture of me in my office on the front cover of it. On the back cover, it had a profile of me and my investment philosophy, plus there were comments about the enclosed tape that had an introductory talk on it. Below that were testimonials of several clients and, in my case, one by Ron Tschetter, who was the executive vice president of Dain Bosworth, Inc., Private Client Group at that time.

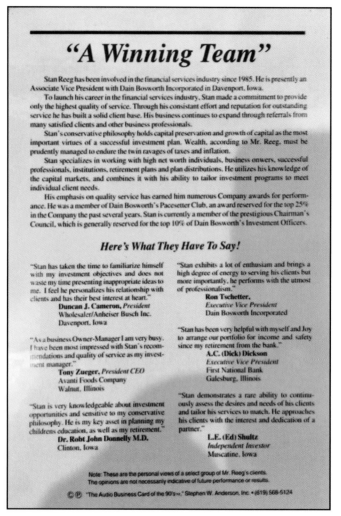

Back side of first Audio Card

I ordered hundreds of them. Some of my clients did testimonials on the back cover of my first audio card, and either they or their heirs are still clients of mine 27 years later. Ron Tschetter was later promoted to president of Dain Bosworth's Private Client Group and in 2006, President George W. Bush named him director of the Peace Corps. That was a great honor for

Ron and his wife Nancy because they both had served in the Peace Corps as young adults.

I gave the audio books to my high net worth clients and centers of influence like CPAs and attorneys who I thought might refer other people to me. I placed my business card inside the audio book, and I included an introduction to the talk on the enclosed cassette tape. On the tape, I gave a short briefing about the types of investing I did, my investment philosophy, and the type of clients with whom I was working. When people listened to the excerpt on the cassette tape, they would relate to how I was working with investment clients and the types of investment concepts we were using and perhaps call me. That was the whole point of creating and distributing the audio card.

In addition, I sent the audio books to prospective clients who had been referred to me. By listening to the tape and reviewing the cover, they would have some insight into my investment philosophy before they came in for their first appointment.

The audio books were a great marketing tool to use with both prospects and higher net worth clients in trying to give me visibility to their heirs and/or their friends, relatives and coworkers. The audio books helped separate myself from the crowd. One of the things I have observed in life is you have to be different than everybody else; if you're going to be the same and use the same approach and methods, you are going to end up being average like the average investment advisor is. In other words, if you always do what you always did, you'll always get what you always got!

Second Audio Business Card

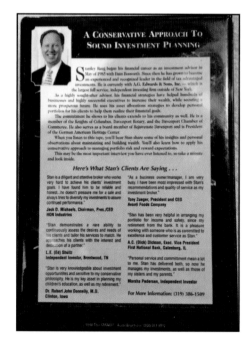

Back side of second Audio Business Card

I was always looking for ways to differentiate my approach in how I managed investment clients and relationships as well as their portfolios.

As I was succeeding, Dain Bosworth hosted many workshops and seminars around the country, especially in Denver and Minneapolis (which is where Dain Bosworth was headquartered). Since I was moving up and growing my business, Jack Stengel, my branch manager in Davenport, was always very supportive of my efforts. He would make sure I got invited to those workshops and seminars. I was certainly eager to attend them because I was always interested in learning how to do things better and faster and in getting bigger results.

Most financial advisors have support staff that we called sales assistants. Initially, I shared a sales assistant named Kelly with three or four other guys in the office. When I had a good month, I would give Kelly a $100 bill. Guess who got support when needed? It seemed common sense to me, but nobody else was doing it.

Later, I told Jack Stengel I needed my own personal assistant and was willing to share in that person's compensation with the office. He added another staff person and assigned Kelly to me as a full-time assistant. She did a great job for me, but after a period of time, I realized I needed someone that had a Series 7 license. The Series 7 is a day-long test you are required to successfully pass in order to buy or sell publicly traded securities like common stocks. In those days, I was trading a lot of stocks. If I was not going to be in the office or if I wasn't available, I needed to have an assistant with a Series 7 license so he/she could take the clients' orders and execute the trades.

Kelly is a great gal, and I told her what I needed. She agreed to study for the Series 7 exam and get the license. The examination in itself is seven-hours long, and it is a pretty challenging test. She took the exam several times and did not pass it. One day I suggested to Jack that when he had support staff or assistant resumes come into the office, I'd appreciate it if he would screen the applicants and keep me in mind, and perhaps interview potential registered sales assistants for me.

When Jack hired a new gal as my primary assistant, Kelly went back to work for the other financial advisors. Recently, I bumped into Kelly at the airport, and she mentioned that she had started at Dain Bosworth in 1985, the same year I did. Here we are decades later and she's still at the same firm. Like many of the other investment companies in America, Dain has since merged into another company, which today is known as RBC Wealth Management. Kelly has done quite well. After I left Dain Bosworth in 1995 to become the A.G. Edwards branch manager, she passed the Series 7 exam and has since become a successful financial advisor.

Getting back to hiring a registered assistant, one day Jack told me he had just interviewed the perfect assistant for me and that, "She's in town for only a couple of days, so you need to be calling her today to establish an interview with her." He went on to say that, "She is living out East and is planning to go back home in a few days." Her plan was to move back to the Quad City area because that is where her parents lived. Her name was Tina.

When Tina came in the following morning for an interview, I had blocked out about one hour for it. After talking with her for an hour, I just kept asking questions because I could not figure out why, with all of her responses and her skills, she did not want to be a financial advisor in her own right. Her response was that she had been an assistant for the past decade and had interviewed several other successful advisors in town the past couple of days, and her goal was to work with and support a "star."

Fortunately, after all those interviews, she chose to work with me. Since she worked with other top-producing financial advisors out on the East Coast, she had a lot of great experience and many good ideas that would help propel my success forward. One of those excellent ideas was for me to get involved in some nonprofit boards in the Quad Cities. Which I did!

That was a rewarding experience in many ways, plus I got to personally know many of the Quad Cities' top business leaders, and they got to know me as well. In 1992 when I hired Tina, I did more than $500,000 of production, and that was the first year I earned more than $200,000 of W-2 income at Dain Bosworth.

In addition to cold calling, I figured out other ways to obtain high net worth clients. Somewhere along the line, I became aware that I had a "nose for money," and that became a great trait to have in our business. I found and developed some clients in ways other than cold calling. The first example is Gene Gunther. Using my Dun and Bradstreet list of executives, I would make cold calls and set up personal appointments with these people at their places of business. In late 1985, I was driving to Galesburg, Illinois, to meet the Cottage Hospital administrator. Galesburg is a 45-minute drive from my office. I noticed on both the drive down and the drive back quite a few large yellow tandem dirt or asphalt hauling trucks. They all looked like new, and they were all very clean. I figured whoever owned that company was either very well off or had borrowed a lot of money.

When I arrived back at the office, I asked my assistant to call Galesburg information to get the number for the Cedar Company, because that was the name I could see on the side of the truck doors. A few days later, I called the number she had obtained, and I asked the receptionist, "Who owns the Cedar Company?" Her response was, "Two brothers, Dale and Gene Gunther, own the company." So I thanked her and hung up the phone.

A couple of days later, I called that same number and asked for Gene Gunther. When he answered the phone, I introduced myself and told him I was a financial advisor at Dain

Bosworth in Davenport, Iowa, and that I had available some AAA-rated insured tax-free municipal bonds and wondered if he would have an interest in tax-free income? He told me he liked investing in higher-yielding insured municipal bonds. I asked him what increments he liked to purchase them in. He told me $25,000 at a time.

A few days later, I called him about an attractive municipal bond offering that we had available, and he decided he would open an account and invest $25,000. I called him again not long after that, and he purchased $25,000 of another issue. As our relationship evolved, he purchased them in even larger increments. Before you know it, Gene had more than $1 million in tax-free municipal bonds with me!

> "It all goes back to my mantra that everything I get involved in must be a "win-win'" for all parties or I won't be a part of it.

I found out later that if Gene Gunther was doing business with you, you had to be exceptional at what you were doing. He referred me to several of his neighbors who were all successful business owners. One of them was the local beverage distributor for Anheuser-Busch and Pepsi products. Another was the president of a local Norwest Bank facility in Galesburg. Here we are 30 years later, and I'm still the advisor for the next generation and, in some cases, succeeding generations of some of those families. I always just treated my clients like I would want to be treated if I were in their shoes. It all goes back to my mantra that everything I get involved in must be a "win-win'" for all parties or I won't be a part of it.

Another longtime client of mine is the Fred and Betty Brown family from Wapello, Iowa. I found Fred's name on one of my Dun and Bradstreet cards. I didn't even know where Wapello was located. I looked on the map and found it down by Burlington, over an hour's drive southwest. When I called Fred, we had a pretty good conversation, and he told me he was running a small machine shop in Wapello. I said, "Some time when I'm down that way, I'd like to stop in and meet you." Shortly thereafter, I did that. I called and told him I was going to be coming through Wapello, as I was going down to Fort Madison to meet with a prominent doctor. Since I had worked in the machine shop at Farmall, when I stopped at his manufacturing facility, I understood what he was producing and the process he was using. The interesting thing about Fred was that when I first met him, he thought diversification was having the best ideas of numerous investment advisors around the country. Once we established a strong relationship, I convinced him to transfer all the assets that he had at other financial service firms to me at Dain Bosworth.

In those days, he wasn't spending all the money he was earning. He had a lot of discretionary cash. I suggested that perhaps at his age, he should start gifting to his three sons. He was not too warm to the idea at first, but in the end it made sense, so he did it. Here we are 30 years later and Fred is expired but his wife Betty is still working with me, and she is in her 90s. Fred's three sons have significant assets invested with me and, to top the story off, his son Doug is still living in Wapello.

Doug worked more than 30 years as a skilled tradesman at Monsanto in Muscatine, Iowa. Because of how Doug feels about how I have treated his family over the years, he has been a great referral resource for me. He has witnessed firsthand how I treat clients and how he has benefited financially. He and his wife Kim have increased their financial net worth significantly by employing my philosophy. He has referred me to many of his coworkers at Monsanto, especially as they are approaching retirement. He would always tell them to call me. As a consequence, many of his associates have transferred their 401K and pension plan balances, which is their lifetime savings and accumulation of wealth, to me.

What I've found over the years is that when people retire, the investment advisor they engage at that time in their lives is generally the professional who is going to manage their assets all through their retirement years.

◇◇◇

After working in the Davenport Branch of Dain Bosworth for a couple of years, I realized that our office was the market maker for Davenport Bank and Trust Company stock. At that time, the Chairman of the Board was V. O. Figge and the bank was one of the top-rated banks in America as to quality and portfolio security.

Since it was a thinly traded stock, and Dain Bosworth was the market-maker, I contacted the State of Iowa Treasurer to obtain a list of all the Davenport Bank and Trust stockholders. The list provided me with their names, addresses, and the number of shares they owned. Once I had the list of shareholders, I requested my assistant to get the phone numbers for each of those people. That was the best prospecting list I could ever have because many of the shareholders were some of the older, wealthy, blue-blood families in the area.

Following that, I started calling them one by one. My script was to introduce myself and then tell them that I knew they were Davenport Bank and Trust shareholders, and my question was, would you be interested in purchasing more shares when they become available? If they weren't interested in purchasing more shares, I would ask them if they would be interested in selling any of their shares. Since the stock had always been a great performer over the past thirty years or so, many of them chose not to sell. But Davenport Bank stock was a premier investment to own and they were always happy to talk about it. I would then ask them, what other types of investments they were interested in. Many of those families were interested in high quality, tax-free municipal bond income. That opened up a lot of doors for me, and I opened up many accounts and developed relationships with quite a few of these shareholders.

Shortly thereafter, I found out that one of the Advisors in my office, Jim Murphy, was selling off shares of Davenport Bank and Trust stock for a major foundation that he was managing assets for in the Davenport area. I told Jim that I was building a list of potential buyers for the Davenport Bank and Trust stock. If any of his clients were interested in selling stock at any time, I would be interested in crossing the sale of shares with one of my purchasers. I opened up many accounts and relationships with some great investors over the years with this approach.

One of the things that I found from that experience is you've got to be thinking outside the box, and you've got to be doing things different than other people. Because, if you're doing the same activities and the same practices as everyone else, you'll get the same results, which means you'll be an average producer, and you'll end up with an average American lifestyle.

While we are talking about investing, another topic I would like to share with you is, in today's world any time you're talking to an investor in the capital markets, they're always talking about 'the market'. Most people don't know what 'the market' is. They think it is the Dow Jones Industrial Average, which only represents thirty of the major companies in the United States, out of over 5,000 companies. Or they may be talking about the S & P 500 which is an index that is comprised of over 500 different stocks. The S & P 500 Index is not an equally weighting of all 500 companies. In other words, companies today like Facebook, Amazon, Google, Netflix, are a larger percentage component of the S & P 500 stocks than many of the other stocks in the S & P 500 Index.

What you will find is it's not equal weighted. It is heavily slanted towards those stocks that the most money is chasing and they can become the larger capitalized companies in America. As an example, back in the late 1990's, the S & P

500 was comprised of all the different industries that make up the economy of America. At the beginning of the nineties, technology stocks were about fifteen percent of the S & P 500 industry weighting. By March 17 of 2000, when the technology stocks peaked and thereafter collapsed, the technology stocks represented approximately thirty-five percent of the S & P 500 Index.

When people talk to me about 'the market', I have to give them a little education and inform them that what 'the market' really is, it's an index that is comprised of publicly traded stocks of many of the great companies of America. These are companies like Amazon, Berkshire Hathaway, Caterpillar, IBM, John Deere, McDonald's, Microsoft, Target, Walgreen's, Walmart, and many others.

When you're talking about 'the market', I think most people are misled. What my clients really own are many of the great companies of the World, and obviously there are times when the stock value of those companies is probably overvalued, because it's like everybody wants to own that stock. Then there are other times when you take, for example, John Deere which like Caterpillar is a cyclical stock can be an underperformer relative to the market. With cyclical industries, there are times when for a couple of years, a stock may really be out of favor and it underperforms the S & P 500 Index. Then you get times where John Deere and Caterpillar have been on a huge run-up in value, and now they are both trading around $170 a share.

The other part of my philosophy is that no matter how high the market is, there are always stocks that are trading at annual lows or major companies where the stock seems to be undervalued relative to the Index. As I'm structuring portfolios for my clients the big thing I am trying to do is: #1, I'm trying to structure the portfolio based on what the client's personal objectives and goals are, and then what I do is I match up their investment portfolio to try and best meet those needs and goals. #2. I'm also trying to make sure, as I structure the portfolio, that we are capturing a significant percentage of the S & P 500 Index, the EAFE Index for Europe, Asia, and foreign equity holdings. As these indexes are going up, I'm trying to capture the majority of that return, but I am also trying to construct the portfolio such that when those indexes go down, that we are not 100 percent cloned to the index, and therefore trying to minimizing the downside risk.

The biggest thing most investors do not understand is that when their portfolio goes down 20 percent, it takes a lot more than 40 percent to get back to even because not only do you have to double what your loss was, but you've also missed out on the time value in the compounding of that money during the recovery time. If you are an investor in the long term over the last ninety years, the S & P 500 has returned 10 percent a year. The main thing is that when the S & P 500 has taken big hits, and we do expect annual corrections based on historical records of about 14 percent some time during each calendar year, you do not want to be 100 percent invested in the S & P 500, especially when the market goes down 15 or 20 percent. By implementing multiple asset classes and multiple styles of equity securities, it should make the years of down performance less painful for you as an Investor!

Another three-generation family I've had the pleasure of working with is the Len Harris family. Len was the founder of Harris Pizza in Rock Island, and back in the late '80s, they had five stores in the Quad Cities. One day in 1989 when I was at Dain Bosworth, we had an office luncheon, and the office manager had ordered Harris Pizzas. Betty and I had always loved Harris Pizza, as we started eating their pizzas back in 1965 when I first met her. It was our favorite pizza.

After the luncheon was over, I asked Debby, our office administrator, if she could check the client files to see if any of our advisors had investment accounts with the Harris family. As it was, no one in our office was working with Len or any of his family members. At that time, a popular income-producing investment was the "hybrid-preferred dividend-paying stocks."

I remember the first time I called Len and presented a bank-preferred offering. It was issued by an eastern bank, and the preferred was paying 12 3/8 percent annual interest. He said he would probably take 50 of them, but first he wanted to come over and see me at the office the next day to discuss the details of the offering. I figured he was just blowing me off, but the next day around 11 a.m., Nancy, the receptionist, buzzed me and said, "There is a Mr. Harris here to see you, and he has another person with him." Nancy brought them back to my office. I had two chairs in my office (by this time, we were in our new office building, and I was in an office rather than out in a cubicle or the bullpen).

Len said, "Can I have one of those chairs in your office?" He put the chair right outside my office door and he told Jerry Spector, who owned Spector Liquors in Rock Island. "You just sit there in that chair and wait for me. I'll be out in a few minutes." Len closed the door and sat down. In those days, he was a big-time smoker. That's when people still smoked in buildings. I did not have an ashtray in my office, as I did not encourage anyone to smoke there. Nevertheless, he seemed like a nice man, so I used a cup for an ashtray and let him smoke a cigarette while we were talking.

I explained all the details of the investment to him, and he wrote a check for $50,000 plus the accrued interest, and we opened his account. A couple of weeks later, I called Len with another offering from an East Coast major listed bank that was offering 12 3/4 percent annual interest on a hybrid preferred. The beauty of these hybrid preferred securities is the issuing entity was not able to call those from our clients until five years after they were issued. So they knew they were going to get that rate of return for a minimum of five years or until they called them. After five years if the bank that issued those securities decided to call them, you knew you were getting all of your original principal back as well. It was a very secure investment.

I continued to call him with other good investments. Previous to investing with me, he had been buying stocks from other financial advisors. He said, "I got screwed by every advisor I've ever worked with." It ended up that he believed I was an ethical and honest person, or at least he sensed that I was an ethical and honest advisor. He also realized I wasn't trying to promote investments that were not in his best interest. Before you know it, he had more than $1 million with me. By the time he and his wife Mary died, they had millions of dollars invested with me.

Once Len trusted me, he always wanted to have breakfast with me. And for him, that was close to noon. He worked the stores late at night and did not get up early in the morning, so noon was breakfast time for him. He told me that if I was going to work as a financial advisor with success-

> "Once Len trusted me, he always wanted to have breakfast with me."

ful people, I needed to wear monogrammed custom-made dress shirts, which is what he always wore. He even brought one of his monogrammed French cuff shirts to my office one day thinking I would wear it. Obviously that did not happen, but that is when I started ordering and wearing custom-fitted shirts.

Another interesting aspect of my relationship with Len was that he would like to come by the office and visit with me frequently. Several times over the years, he brought his young granddaughter Sunday with him. She was a pretty little blonde girl who was still in junior high. He was very proud of Sunday, as she was his only granddaughter. He and Mary only had one daughter, Kathy, and she had two children. Sunday was the youngest, and there was a boy named Ryan. Len wanted Sunday to see what he was doing with his investment money because he wanted her to be a successful investor when she became an adult. Sure enough, today she is a client of mine! She is married and has a hard-working husband who owns and manages a successful business. They have a bright young boy named Aiden. Since I don't plan on ever retiring, I'm sure that at some point in the future I will be working with him as well!

In 1995, We had a prospective client call in to make an appointment to evaluate whether I might be a good financial advisor for them. As we were getting acquainted in that meeting, I was asking them background questions about themselves and their families. They had mentioned that Laurie's (the wife's) parents owned some farm ground on the west end of Davenport. Since her husband Don is a realtor in the Quad Cities, I asked him if he had any idea what the value of that farm ground was. Since it was inside the city, I figured it could be a valuable piece of real estate. I asked them if Laurie's dad had any estate plans in place and if he knew what the value of the farms might be in total. They really did not have any answers, as Laurie had no idea if her dad had done estate planning or not. I suggested for long-term planning needs, it certainly would be good to know what the future held as to possible inheritance and retirement planning.

Before they left my office, I had suggested to them that they might talk to Laurie's parents Albert and Ora Mae about the conversation they had with me that day. I said I would be more than happy in the next meeting to also get acquainted with her parents and see what the future held for all of them. So, Don and Laurie brought her parents along to the next meeting. Albert, being the conservative person he was, valued the farm ground at $2,500 an acre which, from my perspective, was well below market value. At that time, I believe the federal estate tax exemption was $1 million per person, and I thought perhaps just the value of those two properties could exceed that amount. So I suggested to Albert and Ora Mae that they might consider doing some estate planning, and I gave them the name of a couple of attorneys who might be able to help them. What transpired from there is that one of the attorneys suggested they place the farm properties in a family limited partnership since they had three children. The end result is that with further planning and discussions, not only did Don and Laurie become clients of mine, but so did Albert and Ora Mae.

Albert loved investing, and he felt being diversified was working with a number of different advisors and using their best ideas. He also enjoyed tracking the performance of each security on an ongoing basis. Since he was retired, it was something he really was into. He had numerous types of investments and stock holdings with a number of different brokers. I convinced him and Ora Mae that they could have all of their securities at one firm, but the idea of diversification would be to have numerous types of investments in their portfolio. That way they would have one person they had confidence in and that person would understand their entire situation with the whole family portfolio. That all made sense to him, and I suggested he talk to his CPA about my suggestion. After his CPA confirmed that what I suggested made sense, he and Ora Mae consolidated all of their holdings into A.G. Edwards accounts with me.

Fortunately I was able to work with Albert and Ora Mae a number of years before she passed away. Ora Mae was a retired schoolteacher and a very pleasant lady. By the time Ora Mae passed away, I was developing a relationship with their daughter Barbara and her husband Tim, who lived a few hours south of Davenport. The next thing you know, I was doing retirement planning for Barbara and Tim. They were always very complimentary to me because her parents were so pleased with the personal financial advice and planning we had implemented with her parents, as were Don and Laurie.

Tim had been a pharmacist since graduating from college, and they were looking forward to retiring and doing some traveling. Unfortunately neither of them enjoyed good health, so their plan was to enjoy life while they could. They were able to enjoy only a couple years in retirement together because Tim passed away in 2015. Barbara continued to try and enjoy her life as much as possible. She sold her Illinois house and moved to the Quad Cities were she would be closer to her sister Laurie. One of Barbara's favorite things to do was to go to Iowa City and watch the University of Iowa women's basketball team.

Based on Barbara's experience with the Reeg team, she suggested to her daughter Katie that she and her husband Jeff ought to consider doing their investment planning with me. After several consultations with Katie and Jeff, they started investing with me in 2016. The next year, Barbara's other daughter Jennie was planning to get married. In the planning process, we consulted with her and her future husband Jim, and in 2017, they ended up beginning to build an investment portfolio with me. The sad note to this story is that on April 13, 2018, Barbara passed away as a result of cancer. So many lives are impacted by a family member or members dealing with cancer. If you or someone in your family are not dealing with cancer, consider yourselves very lucky.

> "The best things in life aren't things!"

Those are examples of the types of relationships we develop with multiple generations of a family. We always try to make the experience mutually rewarding and to me, it is all about the relationship! It does not make a difference where the heirs or family members live—they are part of the relationship when you are working with me. This whole relationship evolved from one meeting with Don and Laurie and has turned into a multiple generation family relationship. I look forward to serving them and their families many years in the future. That is what motivates me to get up each morning and go to the office most every business day. The best things in life aren't things!

Oldest client to date, Bee Fritz at age 105. She lived to be 108.

I've never met any other really successful stockbroker who worked in a factory. Most of them are college educated, and they come from business backgrounds. For me having had to physically work in a factory setting, I understand the value of a dollar and I hate losing money for a client! The other issue is that I can appreciate the effort some clients have had to make in order to have a living and build up assets to live on in retirement.

When I went through that career assessment class at Clinton Community College in the Spring of 1985, it got me on track to what I was most ideally suited to do in life. Consequently, it was a long way from the factory life—it was more about wanting to be an entrepreneur and being rewarded for my own efforts.

I might not be the smartest guy, but I can outwork others. I put in the effort. It's like my psychologist told me a few years ago when we were walking out of Tommy Bahama's after having lunch in Scottsdale. He said, "Do you know why you're so successful, Stan?" My response was, "Well, there are several reasons." He said, "The real reason is that you set much larger goals than everybody else does, and you go for them, and you make it happen." That is what it is. It's more satisfying to set high goals because the rewards are greater.

◇◇◇

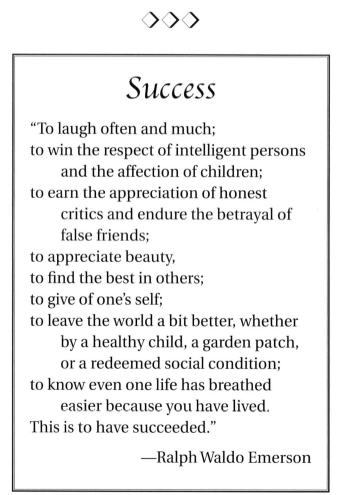

Success

"To laugh often and much;
to win the respect of intelligent persons
    and the affection of children;
to earn the appreciation of honest
    critics and endure the betrayal of
    false friends;
to appreciate beauty,
to find the best in others;
to give of one's self;
to leave the world a bit better, whether
    by a healthy child, a garden patch,
    or a redeemed social condition;
to know even one life has breathed
    easier because you have lived.
This is to have succeeded."

—Ralph Waldo Emerson

Chapter 10

E. F. HUTTON
DIDN'T LISTEN!

Hire Learning

We are all victims or the results of our habits. If things aren't going well for you, you need to change your habits. To expect better results while repeating the same daily habits you are now doing is insanity. Over the last fifty years, I have read hundreds of books. Most of them are biographies, autobiographies, and motivational or books of inspiration. Most of us don't start at the top, but we can learn through other people's experiences and succeed at a faster rate rather than reinventing the wheel.

In all the years I've been in the Investment Business, I've always been in the office more hours than any other advisors. In the first twenty-five years, I was generally the first one in the office and the last one to leave at the end of the day. In the early days, before I left the office in the evening, I always walked around and turned off all the lights in offices that other people had left on. I was thinking like I was an owner, not just the latest employee to join the firm.

The idea of every job is to take ownership. We are each responsible for the results we create. Life is all about choices, and one of my favorite books is 'Your Greatest Power'. I would encourage you to read it. Every day, my goal is to be the best I can be and to try and make a difference in other people's lives.

Some days I don't match up to my goals, but at least I am moving forward or stumbling forward. Ever since my early days when I started in the Investment Business, I have contributed a minimum of ten percent of my earnings to my 401k Plan. Previous to starting my career in finance, I paid the monthly household bills. In order to give me more time to concentrate my energy on building my business, my wife Betty took over paying the monthly bills in 1985 when I started in the Investment Business. My paychecks are direct deposited into my personal investment account each month and she tells me the amount of money she needs to cover the bills on the 10th of each month. I write her a check for that amount plus $500 or $600 for other miscellaneous items. The remaining balance of my monthly paycheck gets invested. I don't care if the markets are at all-time highs or at annual lows. I'm not a believer in timing the market, and history has proven no one can time the markets. Why try to fight the odds? You've got to go with the odds that favor your success.

Since 1926, in other words, over the past ninety years, the S & P 500 Index has averaged over ten percent a year return. It's not about timing. It's about being in the game, or it's about the time in the market. The sooner you get your money invested, the larger the returns will be ten years from now. It's like when we were young kids growing up in Eastern Iowa after a big snowfall. Us kids would go out and want to build a snowman or a snow fort. In order to do that, we would start out with a little compacted baseball-sized snowball and start rolling it around the yard. The next thing you know, you had a two-foot diameter snowball. If you had started out with a larger snowball in the beginning, it just became much larger sooner as you rolled it around the yard, and that is the same principle of why you start investing today not tomorrow or next week!

Another key to becoming a successful investor or building wealth is to minimize the downside risk of your investment portfolio when the S & P 500 Index goes down, which it generally does sometime during each year. It's great to have index performance like the S & P 500 Index or other indexes when they are going up. Over the last twenty-five years we have had an intra-year sell off on the average of about 14.2 percent during the year. Six years out of the last ninety years, the S & P 500 has finished the calendar down in excess of 20 percent down. When your portfolio is down 20 percent, you have to earn more than 40 percent to get back to even, plus you have lost the time value of compounding that money.

Something I've noticed over my lifetime is that when one door closes, another door opens, and it's always a better door, especially if you're a positive thinker. Every experience you are going through today, good, bad, or indifferent, is preparing you for your future. Be an optimist! Many times in life, your greatest opportunity comes from out of left field.

After I was at Dain Bosworth for eight years, I witnessed significant changes at the top corporate management level in our company. I sensed that that would take the company in a different direction and also change the culture of our company. All corporate cultures are constantly changing, as are most other things in our lives today. Ever since my fifth year in the business, I've been in the top ten percent of producers in my investment firm. In addition to the financial compensation earned, we were awarded annual reward trips, many of which were international destinations.

The event that was the fulcrum for me to move on was when we were in Rome, Italy on one of those award trips with Dain Bosworth. The Chairman of the Board stayed at a different resort than the top producers. That never happened with our previous Chairman, who was Dick McFarland.

With the new top corporate executive level priorities, I spent the next two years reviewing possible alternatives to Dain. I really was concentrating on taking my practice the independent route with D. E. Frey, which was headquartered in Denver, Colorado. They were a boutique firm that only hired top producers from major investment firms around the country. I had also enrolled in the Bill Good System several years before that, and attended some of the investment advisory seminars Bill hosted in Salt Lake City. At these conferences, I met many of the most successful Financial Advisors in the Country, as they were not only presenters, but they were participants. You actually got to know them personally as well.

You remember my mother's saying, "Birds of a feather flock together." If you want to be successful, you need to hang out with the brightest and most successful people in your field or business. What you will find is that the more successful the individual is, the more likely they are willing to share their ideas and views with you on how to become better and more successful in your business life.

While continuing my research, I always 'kept the pedal to the metal' in developing my own business, but I was intent on going Independent. Then one day late in 1994, I received a call from a man named Jack Henning from Kansas City. He was the Regional Manager for A. G. Edwards, which was head-quartered in St. Louis. I was aware of the firm, and they did have an office in Davenport, probably for a decade or more before I started in the business. The Davenport office had a reputation in the brokerage community of having average producers at best.

Jack Henning told me that I was selected to be the next new Branch Manager in their office, and my immediate response on that phone call was, "You've got the wrong number." He said, "Well, what are you trying to do?" and I said, "I'm only interested in becoming a million-dollar producer." Jack, being the consummate salesman he was, came back with a classic line, "What makes you think you can't be a million-dollar pro-ducer and a successful Branch Manager at the same time?" That response sure got my attention.

Jack was very insistent that I meet with him at Jumer's Castle Lodge in Bettendorf for breakfast in the next week. I kept tell-ing him, "No, no, no. I'm not interested." I was really busy at the time. I just wanted to get him off the phone. He was so persistent that he would not hang up until I confirmed I would meet with him. So it was a couple of weeks later that we met for breakfast and conversation at Jumer's Castle Lodge in Bettendorf.

After we exchanged greetings and introductions, I told him, "I'm not interested because I'm probably going Independent in this business." Jack was quite persistent and boldly sug-gested that I ought to at least consider going to St. Louis and meeting the corporate executive team. After much resistance from me on that idea, he suggested that since I knew Tim Ska-hill, who was the Branch Manager of the A. G. Edwards office in Waterloo, Iowa, that I should go visit him. By the time we were wrapping up our meeting Jack made the comment, "I have four other people who want to be the Branch Manager and you are my number one choice!" What do I have to do to get you on board?" I told him I was not interested but that I would go visit with Tim to get a perspective about what the Branch Manager role at A.G. Edwards entailed.

The reason I was so reluctant to take on the Branch Manager role was I saw how Jack Stengel, my Dain Bosworth Branch Manager, was always being squeezed and he had one of the more productive offices in the firm at that time. When he would compile the annual revenue and expense budget he would always have to rework it because the firm wanted more revenue from the Branch with lower expenses. I was not willing to spend my time creating budgets and reworking them again. I was most interested in working with clients which is what I still love doing today.

I had originally met Tim Skahill back in 1965, when he was in my Army Reserve Unit in Dubuque. He also had grown up as a neighbor of my wife, and once in a while I would see him when we attended her church by New Melleray Monastery near Dubuque. Once Tim learned I was in the investment Business, periodically he would stop by my office to visit. This was after I had become quite successful at Dain Bosworth. When he was in Davenport, he would stop by and we had some nice visits, but he really never talked much about A. G. Edwards, where he was conducting his business.

In order to pacify Jack and get him off my back, I agreed to give Tim a call. Unbeknownst to me at the time, Tim knew that the current Branch Manager in Davenport was retiring, and Tim is the person that called Jack and told him to hire me!

On my visit to his branch office in Waterloo, we reviewed the duties, the files, the reports, the budgets, and expenses he was responsible for as a Branch Manager. At the conclusion of that visit, he also suggested that I ought to consider going to St. Louis and meeting this Ben Edwards guy.

So the next thing I did was to go to St. Louis to meet Ben Edwards, the Chairman of the Board, and had a wonderful visit with him. Following that visit, my reaction was, "You know what? I could work with people like him for the remainder of my career." He was a friendly, warm, even-tempered leader who you quickly developed confidence and a rapport with. It seemed also that he cared about me as an individual, and that really proved true for all of us Advisors at A. G. Edwards over the years! It is all about the culture and it starts at the top in most all companies.

While I was on the executive floor waiting for one of my appointments, the Executive Secretary announced, "Jack Henning is on the phone." Unbeknownst to me, Jack and the President of A.G. Edwards, talked on the phone almost every day. He was calling Bob to inquire of him how my visit was going and also his perception of me as a potential Producing Branch Manager for A. G. Edwards.

After several more discussions with Jack, I became the new Branch Manager at A. G. Edwards in Davenport. I had worked like a dog to build my book of clients to the level I had at Dain Bosworth, and I didn't want to jeopardize my relationship with my clients.

As I made plans to make my move and move my book of clients to A. G. Edwards, I was very methodical. At that time, I had two assistants. As a team, Tina, Vicky, and I had invested a lot of energy and time into organizing the transition. Tina had worked with other successful advisors on the East Coast and helped them change firms in the past. As it was, Tina and Vicky did a valiant job of getting everything in order and we made the move to A. G. Edwards on June 30, 1995.

Unlike if I was moving to many of the other major wire-house firms in America, A.G. Edwards did not pay a signing bonus. If

I had moved to one of the Wall Street Firms as a Branch Manager, I would have received as much as a seven figure signing bonus. At A. G. Edwards, they didn't do transition or signing bonuses. For the first four months they did guarantee me a minimum monthly income during the time I was transitioning my clients over. They had a very competitive compensation plan and had a generous discount for us employees on their publicly traded stock. Also I had the opportunity to become an Officer in the Company, which was only available for top producing Advisors, and my annual Branch Manager bonuses were based on the production and profitability of my local office. It was a very entrepreneurial way to run a business.

The first day I walked into the office tower by North Park Mall, Jack Henning was there to introduce me to all the employees in a conference room that the office shared with other tenants in the eight story building. I had prepared notes and told the seventeen Financial Advisors how we were going to build the revenue of the office, and it would become noted as the best Investment Firm in the Quad Cities. By now I was convinced A. G. Edwards was the best firm in the country, or I would not have made the decision to move my business and my clients to A. G. Edwards. Previous to that day I had not ever been in the A.G. Edwards office and I was less than impressed with the small offices and the office layout. I found that the previous Branch Manager was more interested in maintaining the bottom line than he was in growing the Branch revenue. Tina and I met immediately after my introductory meeting with the Financial Consultants and staff members. I asked her to find out when the lease was due for expiration or renewal as I made up my mind we weren't staying in that building. Once she did her research she informed me that the lease was due to expire in late 1996.

In March 1998 we signed a ten-year lease on a new office building.

As it turned out, the role of being a Branch Manager for seventeen entrepreneurs and the support staff was a major undertaking. Over the next several years, I took the office from seventeen Financial Advisors down to twelve Financial Advisors, and we more than doubled the revenue and profits of the office.

Being a Branch Manager was a huge challenge for me, and yet it was very rewarding in two ways. One is, I was helping other Financial Advisors be better advisors for their clients. The second, as a Branch Manager, it was financially rewarding if you ran a profitable office. There were years where my Branch Manager bonus exceeded $180,000 in the 1990s, and that was on top of my personal production which generated another $300,000 to $400,000 per year in income.

In our industry, the Branch Manager role is very similar to what it was like for the people that worked at Farmall in the supervisory position. Management is always expecting greater revenue with lower costs, and you are dealing with a bunch of entrepreneurial-type advisors. The Advisors tend to have strong personalities, which means, they are not easily led or directed. From my point of view, it is one of the most challenging roles in our industry.

Shortly after I became the Branch Manager at A.G. Edwards I received a letter of complaint from a renowned doctor that was a client of one of the young advisors in our office. The doctor claimed that his Financial Advisor had made some unauthorized trades in his account. When I called Rick into my office his response was that at his previous firm he did discretionary trading on his client and it was fine. I told him there would be no unauthorized or discretionary trading at A.G. Edwards. And furthermore if I received any more claims of him doing discretionary or unauthorized trades he would be subject to termination. A few weeks later when I was doing the account activity reviews on some of Rick's clients I called one of the lady clients and asked her when was the last time that Rick had contacted her or talked to her on the phone. She told me it was maybe a couple months or more and yet there were recent trades made in her account.

I proceeded to call Rick into my office and told him about the conversation I just had earlier that morning with this particular client. He admitted he had made some discretionary trades in her account without having talked to her. I reminded him that based on our previous conversation about unauthorized or discretionary trades he was subject to being terminated because it was not allowed at A.G. Edwards. I proceeded to inform him that he had a choice and that was to either resign or be terminated. He asked me how long he had to make his decision and I just told him he could sit in my office as long as he wanted. I left my office and closed the door and about five minutes later I came back in and asked him if he had made a decision. He told me he was choosing to resign from A.G. Edwards. Now that I look back on the situation I probably should have just fired him. Hopefully he learned from that experience and became a more ethical advisor going forward.

Another interesting experience I had was when I hired an Advisor who had been referred to me from one of the other major investment firms in town. He was not meeting the firm's minimum goals so I hired him thinking that I could coach him on how to be successful. After hiring him, I placed him on a coaching program and he was required to do a minimum number of activities each day. One of those activities was to make twenty solid contacts per day with prospective clients and to keep a written record of those contacts.

Each week he was to provide me with a written activity report on his daily activities. It appeared like he spent a lot of time on the phone during the day but we were not seeing any business results. As my Assistant Tina and I discussed the situation she got the bright idea to obtain a telephone recording device from our home office in St. Louis. From that we would be able to determine what the content of his conversations were on his phone calls and why he was not getting results. After several days of recording his calls we found that he was calling 900 numbers which were basically sex and pornographic phone-line services. Tina was appalled when we discovered what he was doing. When I called him into my office I never told him about our discovery but I did terminate him for lack of production. And that was the end of him!

I had another well-educated young man apply for a career as a Financial Advisor with A.G. Edwards shortly thereafter. Jim had an undergraduate degree and he also had a Master's degree in Divinity from Harvard University. You would think that a minister that was giving sermons each week to people on how to save your soul would be able to help guide investors on their investment portfolios. But after sending him through all the training and coaching we determined he couldn't ask for the order nor could he make a sale! So needless to say he was not developing any clients nor was he doing any production so I had no choice but to terminate him.

The other issue I was dealing with as the new Branch Manager was that of the seventeen Financial Advisors in the office several of them were not producing enough business or revenue to justify keeping them on as Financial Advisors. In other words the firm was losing money on supporting them. So I implemented coaching procedures and guidelines for them on how they could be more productive and become successful Investment Advisors.

Over the next four years I did everything I could to encourage and coach the low producers on how to build a more successful business and on how to be more valuable to their clients. But as it ended up four or five of them chose to change firms rather than to change their habits. What I learned from that experience is you can coach people that want to be a better Advisor for their clients and be more successful, but you can't help people who are satisfied with mediocrity!

After fifteen years of being a Producing Branch Manager I informed my Regional Manager that I wanted to give up the

Branch Manager role and concentrate solely on working with my clients with full dedication and 100% of my efforts. I remained in the Branch Manager role for almost two more years until the Regional Manager was able to find a candidate to accept the position.

In May 2007 Wachovia Securities announced that they were going to acquire A.G. Edwards. At the time we employees were all in a state of shock because we never believed that A.G. Edwards would be sold to another firm. It was over a 100 year-old firm and had a wonderful culture for not only the Financial Advisors and our staff but also for our clients. Shortly after the announced acquisition we Advisors were informed that we would be receiving a financial incentive to stay with Wachovia Securities. The top producers in the firm were awarded with a check equal to 100% of the preceding twelve months gross production that we generated for the firm. In my case that was in excess of a one million dollar check which was to be treated as a forgivable loan over the next six years.

When A.G. Edwards was acquired by Wachovia Securities, our stock was valued at eighty five dollars per share and by late 2008 when we were in the midst of the Financial Crisis it was down to a couple of dollars per share or less. Unbeknownst to most of us, the year before we were acquired by Wachovia Securities they purchased Golden West Financial Corporation at the peak of the mortgage boom. Golden West was one of those California based companies that had arranged housing mortgages for people with little or no down payment and in some cases financed in excess of 100% of the appraised value! When the mortgage crisis hit in 2008 it dramatically impacted Wachovia's balance sheet. By late 2008 we advisors weren't sure what the future held for us or even if we would have a job! It was pretty unnerving because we were at the mercy of the regulators. In fact for about twelve hours it appeared like we were going to be owned by Citigroup. Then on December 31, 2008, we were acquired by Wells Fargo and named Wells Fargo Advisors.

Being an Investment Advisor with Wells Fargo Advisors was a totally different experience. Wells Fargo may have had a good bank model but they certainly didn't understand the investment advisory business. I believe the executive level management viewed us 15,000 Financial Advisors as 15,000 outlets for their bank products including loans, mortgages, lines of credit, credit cards and deposit accounts. After going through all of these changes many Financial Advisors decided to move their practices to other firms were they felt the culture would be more supportive of how they were trying to add value to their client relationships. Consequently, in the fall of 2009 Wells Fargo Advisors came out with what most people would consider a Retention Bonus. This bonus was going to be treated like the Wachovia retention award as a forgivable loan over the next nine years. So in February 2010 Wells Fargo gave me a bonus that was in excess of $600,000 and since it was treated as a forgivable loan each month you earned back the bonus over the next nine years.

After going through all of these mergers and acquisitions the culture was nothing like what we had experienced previously at A.G. Edwards. By this time my son Todd had become quite successful in the Investment Business as well. Both he and I were disillusioned with how Wells Fargo Advisors was managing the investment business so we decided we needed to move our practice to a firm that appreciated the type of investment advisory business we had built and would support us in this endeavor to serve our clients.

Over the previous twenty eight years I had made a lot of observations about how other firms in the Financial Services Business operated. We were not looking to get a huge payday, what we were looking for is to experience a culture that was similar to what A.G. Edwards was years previously. We were looking for a firm where you were supported and treated as an important person in their business. I visited a number of different investment firms and we looked at establishing our own investment advisory firm as an independent investment advisory practice.

In the end we chose to move our business and clients to Robert W. Baird which was a 95-year-old company at the time because it is more like a boutique investment firm where you had your own brand but were supported by a very experienced full-service investment firm. It is an employee-owned firm where every employee has the opportunity to own stock.

When we visited Baird headquarters in Milwaukee and met some of the top leaders like Paul Purcell who is the Chairman of the Board and other top management level people it just felt good! It reminded me of my experience in St. Louis when I met Ben Edwards back in 1995. Baird's mission is 'to provide the best financial advice and service to our clients and to be the best place to work for our associates'. Each year since 2004 Baird has been recognized as 'one of Fortune's 100 Best Companies in America to work for'. Generally Baird has been in the top 15 which tells you a lot about the culture of our company.

You remember the $600,000 plus Retention Bonus I was awarded by Wells Fargo Advisors back in 2010. Since I was not even half way into the nine years I had to pay back about $350,000 of it to Wells Fargo. The good news is that my clients and I are in a much better place!

Quad City Times feature, Winter, 1998

Chapter 11

<u>INVESTMENTS:</u>

THE PROMISE OF A LOVER, THE PERFORMANCE OF A HUSBAND

If There Was a Sponge that Cleaned Up Broken Dreams, Woolworth's Would Still Be In Business

THE ODDS WERE GOOD,
BUT THE GOODS WERE ODD

This venture was my brother Mike's idea when legalized gambling opened up in Cripple Creek, Colorado. It was one of the first Colorado communities where gambling was allowed. Mike was doing construction work in Cripple Creek with Tri-Star Masonry. They were rehabbing some buildings that were being converted into casinos. Many of these places were only 25-foot storefronts. He said, "You know what, Stan? We've got an opportunity here to get rich. We're going to build the biggest casino in Cripple Creek."

We bought a whole city block on contract from a family who had lived in Cripple Creek for years and years. We were paying $8,500 a month on contract.

Many of our family members begged and borrowed to put in as much money as they could. I invested $105,000 in the deal in 1992. Mike formed one company, which was called Iowa Cripple Creek LLC. Another guy who was going to be our partner in the deal was Ron Ortner. Ortner was a hotshot who supposedly had a lot of wealthy friends. When it was time for Ortner and his partners to bring money in, Ortner kept saying, "I've got to get these guys to come in. I've got to get these guys to come in." Well, unbeknownst to us, he was blowing the money. My brother was moving ahead as if the deal was going to happen. We did all of the infrastructure, the big huge grease tank traps you need for restaurants, the foundation and everything. Ron Ortner was not coming up with the money he promised us. Mike said, "Who are a couple of your largest investors?" Mike got the names of these investors and called each one. Well, they had given Ortner all kinds of money, and he was blowing it.

Mike decided, "We can't fund this whole thing ourselves. We're not going to be able to borrow that many millions of dollars." Consequently, he called Ortner and had a "Come to

Jesus" talk. Ortner would have to come up with the money or there were going to be serious consequences. It ended up that he did not come up with any money. My brother decided we had better figure out how to sell this.

Ortner was involved with the Seventh-Day Adventist Church. My brother had built a couple of churches for them. Ortner turned out to be a con man. Ortner hooked the churches up with my brothers, and my brothers built the churches. Then Ortner got into doing country and western concert promotions. My brother had invested in a couple of those, and they maybe broke even at best. Ortner always talked like he had a lot of friends with a lot of money. "If you ever come up with a great idea, I will be able to get some partners and do it." That's how he ended up becoming our 50 percent partner in what originally was the Grand National Hotel and Casino.

This process was going on for several years. My brother Mort sold the Grand National Hotel and Casino to a group of investors, which was called Triple Eagle Ventures LLC. He had the right idea, but we had the wrong partner. Ortner later on committed suicide because he had defrauded so many of his friends out of money. Today it is the largest hotel and casino in Cripple Creek. It's called Double Eagle Hotel and Casino. I would have held 17.1 percent of that venture.

If Ortner would have come through with what he promised, we would have ended up with the biggest and most profitable casino in Cripple Creek. In the end, my brother sold it to another party. None of us relatives lost money on the deal. We had every penny we could come up with invested, so that was a nervous one.

The lesson here is to be careful who you bring in for partners. You had better know them. You just don't take them at face value. You need to do your homework and investigate their backgrounds and their associates, partners and investors.

THERE WAS ROOM AT THE INN—A LOT OF ROOM!

In 2004, people approached me about investing in a hotel in Eldridge, Iowa. It's really the only hotel in Eldridge and was built in 2001. A partner was getting divorced, and they wanted somebody to take over his ownership interest. I invested $35,000 in it for 4.15 percent ownership. Over time, we had capital calls and had to add more money. By April 2008, the occupancy was not high enough to make any money. We had been feeding it. We found a buyer. Not only did I have $40,000 in, but when we got to the closing table, we did not have enough capital to cover the loan. All us partners had to write more checks—my share was $7,301.77. It ended up being a total loss. My loss on that four-year investment was $55,251.77.

When the hotel was built in 2001, John Deere was putting up their dealers and clients in the hotel. The Deere Mount Joy facility is just down the road from the hotel, but John Deere changed their policy. When they entertained clients at hotels, they wanted the hotels to have a full bar, and we did not have a full bar and restaurant. They quit using us, and that killed our daily occupancy rate. That's why that one went south in a hurry.

It's now a Quality Inn. I still have an attachment to it because I want it to do well. It looks like they may be doing all right. You need a 60 percent occupancy to make money or break even.

Again, I didn't do my homework ahead of time. The average occupancy in the Quad Cities was 54 percent. You are not going to make money or even break even when the whole community is at 54 percent occupancy. There's no way the numbers work. From that deal, I learned to do more homework before investing. Success has a thousand fathers; failure is an orphan.

THIS HAPPENED IN SIERRA VISTA—
I DIDN'T KNOW ANYTHING HAPPENED IN SIERRA VISTA

The next project was a real estate limited partnership called "Sierra Vista." My son Todd and I were minor partners. This was October 2005, when things were rolling. We bought 1,811 acres in an area in Arizona called Sierra Vista. It was residential land in Cochise County. It made a lot of sense. The partners we invested with had a lot of experience in real estate. By December 2008 and the financial crisis, it was a zero. They just dissolved the partnership because the general partners didn't have enough money to cover the mortgages. We lost the entire $50,000 we invested. The lesson I learned there is when everything is hot, don't touch it.

The financial crash was blamed on the financial services industry, but it really was the government. Back in the 1990s, President Clinton wanted everybody in America to have the ability to own a house. They made the mortgage companies, Freddie Mac and all the agencies lower the lending criteria. People were allowed to buy houses or real estate with nothing down. The reality is that these companies overlent money. The people they were lending to were not qualified credit risks. Consequently, they lowered the qualifications, but not everyone is built to own a home. Many people are renters for a reason. They don't want to be responsible or to take care of something. They shouldn't be homeowners. The whole adage is "No skin in the game. What have you got to lose?"

It's the same thing that happened in the late 1970s with Federal Farm Credit. Agencies were pushed to lend money to farmers and encourage them to buy second and third farms and leverage up. Then we had the agriculture crisis, when prices all went to pot.

IF YOU AIN'T GOT DIGITAL, YOU AIN'T GOT SQUAT

In July 2011, I invested in a Texas-based company that was digital switch. They were working with Oracle, the big tech company. The company was called IPCelerate, Inc. I invested $200,000 in it. I'm getting smarter now. It was a really good friend of mine who had been in it from the time they originally founded the company, and he said, "This is an awesome deal.

They've got the deal going with Oracle. This thing is going to work out."

I ended up with 133,333 preferred shares. In December 2017, it went to zero. That one took only a few years to go to zero. I learned that you can invest with friends, but you need to know what you're investing in.

WE WERE GOING TO ADVERTISE A NEW MCDONALD'S PRODUCT FOR UNDER A BUCK: McDEER NUGGETS

The next one I did was through a car friend of mine from Arizona. They had this great idea called Smart Screen Media. They were testing these advertising TV screens in McDonald's locations. I invested $100,000 in the spring of 2014. At first, I was getting calls from the partners. They were saying, "Oh, this is great. We're testing in this store and that store."

Of course, I had the prospectus, which is a bunch of paper really, but in January 2018, that turned into zero. I'm not sure what happened. The president of the company bailed. I think they were burning up all of the capital on people's salaries rather than development. The whole idea made sense. At many gas stations today, you see these screens at gas pumps. It's the same concept as what we were going to do at McDonald's stores. They were in a lot of McDonald's stores, but obviously the leadership at McDonald's said, "Hey, we're not doing this." That was the end of that company because that's what we were banking on. The story here is that you don't bank on just one customer or one business model.

MAYBE THE RIVER BANDITS WERE APTLY NAMED AFTER ALL

The next project is a sweetheart: the Quad Cities River Bandits minor league baseball team. In 2000, the Krause family from Des Moines was in the process of purchasing the Quad Cities River Bandits...later the Quad Cities Swing, and years later, they changed it back to the Quad Cities River Bandits. They are a Single A baseball team. The Krauses invited a group of successful Quad Cities business people to invest. I figured that the Jay Ingrams and the Mike Duffys of the world were a lot smarter than I was. If they were investing in it, it had to be a good investment. We invested in early 2000. I don't have all the numbers because I destroyed everything. I was so upset when this thing went belly up on our part that I just destroyed all the information once I filed taxes.

In 2003, Kevin Krause became the general manager. He previously had minor league sports franchises that had failed in Cedar Rapids and western Washington state. In 2003, we completely renovated the whole stadium. It was an old stadium, and we renovated it to state of the art. We

> "It was enough to make Kurt Warner curse."

built new locker rooms, expanded the stadium, built the berm around the stadium, installed a big media scoreboard and invested a lot of money.

The city didn't seem to want to work with Kevin Krause. There was a committee of three of us who started to work with Craig Malin, the city manager in Davenport, to negotiate to where we would make more money.

The bottom line is, the investors never made any money. The city ended up with a new stadium. The franchise was sold to new ownership in 2007. All of us investors took a total loss. How much money Krause made, I don't know. The city of Davenport ended up with a state-of-the-art baseball stadium, and Krause moved back to Des Moines, and that's the end of that one. The lesson learned is that no matter how sophisticated or successful the people who you are investing with are, you've got to do your own homework.

After we sold out, the franchise supposedly was sold for $4.5 million. I had some good partners there, but we got screwed.

Modern Woodmen Insurance contributed to have the naming rights to the stadium. The place is a huge success today. It's a great venue. That's just the way it goes.

TechKnow

In 1998, Dr. Michael Giudici, a Quad Cities electrophysiologist, bought a large farm on the north side of the Quad Cities. He turned it into the Iowa Research Commerce and Technology Park. He wanted to do that for the city of Davenport. Doc had started Greenway Habitat, which planted thousands and thousands of trees around the Davenport/Bettendorf area over 20 years.

Anyhow, Dr. Giudici came up with the tech park idea, and he developed it. He put in the infrastructure: the drainage, the curbs, the gutters and the boulevard, and he planted trees in the center of the boulevard. He had brought some other doctors in as limited partners. He was the general partner. He was spending $30,000 a month on interest alone because the interest rates were high in those days. I felt bad for him. I invested $60,000 into that enterprise, and that gave me maybe 2 percent of the total.

Several important buildings have been built there over the years. You have to drive in there: It's a really cool park. Mike is an honorable guy. He ended up selling the remaining part of the development off. In early 2013, he paid me back $80,000.

I put $60,000 in in 2001, and 12 years later, I walked out with $80,000. I was happy as a pig eating dingoes.

So, on these investments, I shanked some and didn't get a mulligan on any, but I learned a few nuggets: (1) The best way to make money in a Gold Rush is to be the one selling the shovels; (2) Success consists of going from failure to failure without loss of enthusiasm; (3) It's always good news until it ain't; and (4) 60 percent of the time I'm right 100 percent of the time.

Chapter 12

ARIZONA—
LOVE AT FIRST SITE

I Like It, I Love It,
I Want Some More Of It

ARIZONA REAL ESTATE

Back in 1999, our son Todd was living in Phoenix. He suggested that I should be involved in the Arizona real estate market. He was thinking someday I would want to be living in The Valley of the Sun. Furthermore, Arizona real estate is a much better investment than Iowa real estate. In Iowa, you're lucky if the value of your home or property increases at the rate of inflation.

Todd introduced us to a real estate agent, Grant Mastre, in Scottsdale. Grant had built a house for Todd a few years before.

A few years later, Todd sold that house and purchased another house in McCormick Ranch, an upscale Scottsdale development. Todd gutted that house, remodeled it, added more rooms, and added a three-car garage. He and Jodi lived in it only a few years because Grant called Todd and said he had a prospect who wanted to see the inside of the house. When the lady viewed the house and grounds, she had to have the property. Todd and Jodi sold it for more than $300 per square foot, which was the most money per square foot any house in McCormick Ranch had ever sold for.

A few months before that, Todd was working at the A.G. Edwards office in Scottsdale when Sean, one of the advisors, told Todd that he had an elderly client who deposited funds into her account that were proceeds from the sale of her house in Paradise Valley. She also told Sean that she still had the adjoining lot for sale. Todd asked Sean where it was located and immediately left the office to see the lot, which was in the foothills of Mummy Mountain. Todd was quite taken by the property.

The owner was a retired realtor and was selling it on her own, as she did not want to officially list it. To make a long story short, with Grant's assistance, Todd owned the property before any of the neighbors knew it was for sale. Furthermore, he had purchased it below market rate for lots in Paradise Valley because he was a cash buyer. At that point, he and Jodi were trying to determine what style of home they would like to live in. They both desired a modern style home. They hired an architect who specialized in those types of structures and proceeded over the next few months to design a residence that fit their personal preferences. Once they finalized the design, they started construction, which took more than a year to complete. I would say it has a lot of Frank Lloyd Wright influence in its colors and design. It is a beautiful home surrounded by all native Arizona plants and landscaping.

Grant has turned out to be a great friend to our family. Grant loves the Gainey Ranch community in Scottsdale and has lived in numerous properties in the Enclave at Gainey Ranch. We really didn't have a clue where we should be buying investment property in Arizona. Grant introduced us to Gainey Ranch.

The first time we viewed real estate with him, we looked at condominiums, townhomes, and houses. After one day of shopping, we had identified a condominium in Gainey Ranch that we really liked. We thought it could be a good investment property. With Grant's assistance, we made an offer to the Chicago owner. That property was maybe only six years old at the time, but it had been totally remodeled and rebuilt with new cabinets, fresh plaster board, and new floors and trim. The owner lived in Chicago and one day, the security people noticed that there was water running out the front door. The sprinkler system went bad, and water virtually destroyed the interior of that condo.

The owner had insurance and rebuilt the whole unit, so it was like brand new. When Betty and I visited it, we thought it was nice since it had a golf course view, and it would be something that we would be willing to live in. We thought it would make a good investment property and we could find renters.

We purchased that property in 2000. We rented it to a lady who was in the process of building a luxurious home in Desert Mountain, north of Scottsdale. She ended up in a lawsuit with her builder because he wasn't delivering what he had promised. The cost and the length of the construction just continued to go on and on. Finally, after three years, she moved into her new home, which left us vacant about two months. Grant found a doctor who was interested in leasing the condo until he found something to buy. He and his wife were in that property for the next three years.

In 2006, I saw that real estate values in Arizona had escalated significantly. I thought maybe the market was overvalued. I was in St. Louis at a seminar, and one of the topics that was discussed at length was that everything goes through cycles. There are times when things are undervalued, and there are times when investments are overvalued. I realized with the Arizona real estate market having been as hot as it was, maybe it was time to take a profit. When I arrived back in the Quad Cities from St. Louis, I decided to go in my office that Saturday afternoon to get Grant's telephone number.

I called Grant and asked, "How much do you think you could sell my Gainey Ranch condominium for?" and he said, "Well, I think I could get $600,000 for it." I said, "Really?" He said yes. I said, "Sell it." His response was, "Really? Why do you want to sell it?" and I said, "I think it's overvalued, and prices in real estate will probably have a significant sell off at some point in the future." I said, "I will come back into the Gainey Ranch area and buy something else at that time when I feel it's a better value."

We had paid $310,000 for that unit in 2000, and in less than 60 days after Grant listed the property, it sold. We closed on it and sold it for $575,000 in 2006. Plus, we had it rented out for all but two months out of the six years. It was a great investment.

What wasn't so great is what I did with the proceeds. I paid a significant amount of taxes to Uncle Sam, and I invested the remainder in the stock market. Then in 2008 and 2009 when the stock market went through a major correction, I lost most of the profit I made on that property.

One August day in 2010, when we were in Scottsdale visiting Todd, Jodi, and the girls, Grant called me. Betty and I had rented a van, and we were all driving over to San Diego's Coronado Island to stay at the del Coronado Hotel for a few days with Todd and his family. We were also going to spend some time downtown in the Gaslight District of San Diego.

Grant thought we had seen the bottom of the real estate market in the Enclave in Gainey Ranch. He felt that way because Canadian buyers were paying cash for Gainey Ranch properties, and there were minimal houses available for sale. He said, "If you're looking for value, now is probably the time to get in the Scottsdale market."

> "If you're looking for value, now is probably the time to get in the Scottsdale market."

That was a Monday. We were going to be in San Diego until Thursday evening late. I said, "Betty and I are flying back to the Quad Cities on the weekend. You arrange showings, and we will spend all day Friday with you." Friday morning, we looked at a house in the neighborhood. It was a house that needed a total renovation, and I didn't want anything like that.

He then showed us a couple of townhouses. I said, "We're not interested in those." Following that, he showed us a few condominiums, and we weren't particularly enamored with any of those properties. Grant could sense that, so he said, "I've got another house I would like you to look at, but I would have to call the owners and see if we might be able to see it today." I said, "Well, that's fine with us." We had dedicated the day to be viewing properties anyway.

He called the owners, and they said they were going to have guests in to play cards that afternoon. The owners were in their early 90s and had just celebrated their 65th wedding anniversary. They were planning to move into a new senior citizens' development in Scottsdale. What we didn't know is they had been trying to sell this house for the last 2 1/2 years. They originally listed it in 2007 and because of the declining real estate values, they kept lowering the asking price. They still could not get it sold because houses weren't selling, and if they were selling, it was at much lower prices.

Consequently, they had taken the house off the market for a few months. About a week before Grant called us, they relisted the property. Most people didn't know the house was for sale yet. Grant was aware because he lived a few houses down the street. The price from the time they initially listed the house until we saw it, went down 40 percent.

We walked through the house with Grant and our son Todd. Todd toured the property with us because he had a pretty good eye on Arizona real estate market and the values. After we walked through the house, we were standing in the back-yard, and I said to Grant, "I am ready to put an offer in on this house. I love it." I said, "I see these people built it in 1991, and it's in great condition, but the core is very outdated. I can see at some point we're going to have to spend some money updating it and making it more modern," to which he agreed.

After three weeks of negotiating, we ended up buying the property. The house has appreciated significantly in value since we bought it. We pretty much hit the bottom of the real estate housing market in 2010.

About two weeks after the closing, Grant called me and said, "Would you be interested in renting your house out?" I said, "Oh, I don't know about that." I said, "What kind of monthly rent would we be able to lease it out for?" He said, "I think I could get you $3,500 a month." I said, "Is that $3,500 a month in the winter season or is that year round?" He said, "No, that would be year round." I said, "Rent it out!"

The following week, he leased it out for the next two years. Consequently, we didn't initiate any improvement on the property. After the tenant had been in the house for two years, he wanted to lease it another year. We responded, "No. We're getting at the stage in our life where we want to start using the property ourselves."

When the lease expired, we hired Grant to quarterback the total renovation of the house. We knocked out walls, cut openings in walls, and we took out the kitchen ceiling. We did a total renovation and a new layout of the living areas. Previous to getting in the real estate business, Grant was an interior designer. He has a great eye and a knack for how to utilize space to the maximum and make it attractive at the same time.

In 2013, we spent a good portion of the year having the house renovated. In 2014, we decided we were going to spend our winters in Arizona. That's what we've done since. It's been a great experience, and we love living in the Enclave. We love the neighborhood and the house may now have appreciated back up to the original 2007 asking price.

Chapter 13

ON THE ROAD AGAIN

'Tis Better to Travel Well
Than to Arrive First

Many times when I am talking to clients or friends about where I am traveling to next, they ask "Why are you going there?" And generally it is someplace in the third world or some destination that most Americans don't travel to. Our International travel all started back in the summer of 1984 when we went to Europe for five weeks and two days with the boys. At that time Todd was age sixteen and Eric was twelve years of age. That was the first time we had been outside of the Continental United States. On that trip we traveled Switzerland, Germany, France, Austria, Italy, Monaco and Luxembourg. We realized that we did not have any old buildings in America compared to the European structures. We were fascinated and impressed with the architecture and the antiquity of some of these buildings. In other words we were captivated by the uniqueness.

So that is one of the main reasons why we have done a lot of international travel over the last thirty years or so. Many of the most exciting International trips we have experienced are because of us having met Lynn Soli back in 1998 when we were on the Pinnacle Award trip with A.G. Edwards in New Zealand.

The Pinnacle Trip was a recognition trip that A.G. Edwards provided to the top hundred producers at A.G. Edwards in those days. Since I had qualified for the New Zealand trip, Betty and I decided to go early and spend five days in and around Sydney, Australia. So at that point that was the longest flight we had ever been on because we left Los Angeles on a Boeing 747 and arrived fifteen hours and thirty minutes later in Sydney. The Maritz travel crew who coordinated the trip for AGE made reservations for us at a nice hotel in downtown Sydney.

While we were in Sydney we did a number of tours out to the Blue Mountains, the former Olympic Stadium site, we also visited Bondi Beach which is world-renowned for its waves and surfing, plus we spent part of a day visiting the Royal Sydney Golf Club and touring the course which is where Ike Hurning the current Grounds Superintendent of Springbrook Country Club Golf Course in DeWitt, Iowa formerly worked.

Following that we flew over to Auckland, New Zealand where we spent a few days with the rest of the attendees. We next flew to Queenstown where we stayed for the next four or five days in a very nice hotel. From there each day we did some interesting day trips. One day we drove out south of Queenstown for a couple of hours on a bus and at some point we pulled up to an airfield where they had a number of small airplanes that had cabin space for anywhere from four to ten passengers. Betty and I ended up flying down to the Fjords in an eight passenger plane with Ben and Joan Edwards. At that time Ben was the Chairman of the Board at A.G. Edwards.

Upon arriving back to our hotel from that day trip, Betty told me she thought that the jewelry she had left on the top of the dresser was missing. I suggested to her that it probably was stuck in one of the drawers or perhaps she placed it in the safe. After searching everywhere we could think of in our Hotel room, she decided we ought to talk to the Maritz staff people that were accompanying us on the trip. So we proceeded to go down to their hospitality desk and that is where we met Lynn Soli.

Betty explained to Lynn that she felt she had left jewelry on top of the dresser that morning before we went on tour and when we arrived back in our room that afternoon it was not there. She told her we had looked high and low with no results of being able to find the jewelry. So with Lynn being the detail person she is, she volunteered to come up to our room to look one more time. As it was there was no jewelry found so Lynn next proceeded to report the missing jewelry to the hotel management. The hotel manager told Lynn they had never had any items stolen from any of the rooms previously and no one had ever reported any losses to him.

After that conversation Lynn told Betty that she knew enough about what happened that she would follow up and continue to investigate the situation and to get a result. Fortunately it was not high dollar fine jewelry but it was jewelry that had some sentimental value to Betty. During the remainder of our stay at that hotel Lynn continue to pursue the mystery of the situation. On the last day when we were getting ready to leave since the jewelry was never found Lynn negotiated with the hotel management to agree to at least compensate Betty with a $300 settlement for the inconvenience.

Betty got to know Lynn because of this incident and she really appreciated Lynn's persistence in trying to resolve the situation to the best of her ability. Betty was very appreciative of Lynn's efforts and so during the whole affair they got personally acquainted and she witnessed Lynn's dedication to the participants that had joined us on that trip. After we arrived back home we kept in touch with Lynn and over the next several years we attended more Pinnacle Award trips with Maritz and Lynn.

Maybe a year after getting back home from New Zealand, Betty received a phone call from the Constable of Queenstown and he informed her that they had recovered her and other hotel guest's jewelry from a former hotel employee. The Constable told her that there would be a hearing and perhaps a trial but at the end of the investigation or inquiry she would at some point get her jewelry back. So maybe ten months later someone from the Constable's office called to inform Betty that the case was settled and that her jewelry would be shipped to our residence and they just wanted to verify our mailing address. A week or so later Betty did get back all her pieces of jewelry.

Then in 2004 Lynn organized her first what she called 'Friends and Family' trip. We were pleased when she invited us to join her on a 2005 trip to South America and Peru. On that trip there were twenty two of us travelers. We visited Cusco, Lake Titicaca which is the highest freshwater lake in the world at 12500 feet of elevation, and many other historic sites with Machu Picchu being the highlight. We arrived there by narrow gauge railroad from Cusco then we took a shuttle bus up to the historic site and toured the grounds. The following morning ten of us took a shuttle from our resort up to the historic ground and then we all hiked up to the Sun Gate pass. As we were hiking up through the clouds I thought we were in for a big disappointment. Sure enough when we got to the Sun Gate Summit we were still in the clouds. Those who brought along coffee started sipping their coffee and visiting. Maybe ten or fifteen minutes later you could feel a little breeze coming through the Pass. Next thing you know the breeze blew the cloud cover out and we could see right down into Machu Picchu. The view was incredibly spectacular! It was a picture like you will never see in a travel brochure, it was majestic! After a while our group proceeded to hike back down the steps to Machu Picchu where we were joined by the remainder of our tour group that had slept in.

That day when we were at Machu Picchu I told Lynn, the next time I come back to visit Machu Picchu I am going to hike the Inca Trail in to the site in order to feel like I deserved the right to witness that spectacular view again!

> "It was a picture like you will never see in a travel brochure, it was majestic!"

We have been on many other trips with Lynn over the years to such places such as South Africa, China and Tibet, Budapest, and Argentina. In 2008 we toured Thailand, Cambodia and Burma with her. In 2009 we visited South America again. We flew into Santiago, Chile and then two hours later we flew 2400 miles East over the Pacific Ocean to Easter Island, 2010 we were in Morocco, 2011 we were in Portugal with her, 2013 we were in Sweden and Russia, in 2016 we traveled to Ecuador and the Galapagos Islands with her and then in 2017, she decided to organize another trip back to Peru and Machu Picchu.

As Lynn was organizing the Machu Picchu portion of the trip I told her I would really like to have someone join me on doing the one day hike into Machu Picchu. As the summer passed I knew there were going to be thirty eight of us going to Peru in the fall, so I figured someone else certainly would want to do the Inca Trail hike with me. As the months passed no one expressed any interest.

As the summer wound down one of the couples that go on Lynn's trips with us was hosting a celebration at their house in Milwaukee. After we arrived at the party I learned that there was also a two-day charity bicycle ride around the Milwaukee area. Paul Buskey a friend of mine from Sarasota, Florida and his wife Tammy had flown into town, as Tammy was planning to participate in the bicycle ride. Paul and Tammy were also planning to travel to Peru and Machu Picchu with us in October. Over dinner and wine I was telling Tammy my dilemma, that Lynn and I could not come up with anyone to accompany me on the Inca Trail hike into Machu Picchu. I am not sure if she was feeling sorry for me or what, but she said "I'll do the hike with you." Obviously I was excited, because now I was not going to be hiking that day long historic trail by myself. I knew Tammy would be good company as well. I always felt that when you are viewing wonders of the world the experience is much more meaningful if you are sharing the view with someone else.

Once we got back home I realized I had better get serious about training for this Inca Trail hike as I knew it was not going to be like a 'walk in the park'. So my morning exercise program consisted of walking the hills around our area as well as riding my bike and using a CrossFit training box that I repeatedly stepped up and down off of fifty to one hundred times several times a week just to condition my legs for climbing the stairs and the elevation on the Inca Trail. I checked in with Tammy and she was telling me that she was riding her bike thirteen miles a day plus she was going to the gym and working out to get prepared for the hike.

When we arrived in Peru the weather was generally nice and we spent the first few days in the Sacred Valley. The day the group was to visit Machu Picchu everyone else was taking the train from Cusco into Machu Picchu. Tammy and I walked down to the train station with our guide who met us at the hotel. We rode a narrow gauge train for maybe an hour outside of Cusco towards Machu Picchu. When the train stopped we walked across the swinging rope and wood plank bridge over a stream. We stopped there to use the facilities and get prepared for our hike. We took a few pictures and then our guide introduced us to our Sherpa who was going to carry our extra clothing, water supply, and lunch for us in his backpack. The weather was perfect for a hike that morning as it was above fifty degrees when we got off the train.

Stan Reeg on the Inca Trail. Locals sometimes spell it "Inka".

We started the hike with a lot of enthusiasm and walked around the side of five or six different mountains through some very interesting historical sites that you will only see if you hike the trail yourself. We would hike up a few hundred feet and then walk back down a few hundred feet and then back up. Some of the steps on the trail were maybe five or six inches high while in other places they were twelve to fourteen inches high. In some areas the trail was a very narrow pathway with a cliff immediately below you so you needed to really watch every step. The hike was much more challenging than I had expected but because of our training the previous few months we were prepared for it. The whole experience ended up being a very exciting adventure and I'm glad we did it!

The background of the previous photo.

All in all we hiked seven hours over eight and one half miles at elevations from 5,000 to 7,000 feet altitude. Our guide was very informative and we did take some time to take photos and enjoy the views. When we arrived at the Sun Gate Pass where I had hiked to twelve years earlier with Lynn and the group we were rewarded with the same incredible view. As we hiked down the trail into those historic grounds, periodically we would stop as our guide would fill us in on the history with anecdotes about Machu Picchu. Once we arrived at the historic site he spent another two hours giving explanations and perspectives as we toured all around the historic site.

Inca Trail hikers

If you are ever to go to Peru, even if you don't like to hike or you don't want to travel on the Inca Trail, which I realize most tourists don't you want to do, be sure to visit Machu Picchu and tour the historic grounds with a guide! It is something you will never regret.

Tammy Burns and Stan Reeg with Machu Picchu in the background.

Betty and I did another trip with Lynn and her husband Bruce in 2016. It was the type of trip I dreamed about for years. I thought it would be fun to stay in a Villa around Siena, Italy, rent a car for a week and each day tour one of the scenic old walled towns in the Tuscany wine region. The seed was planted when we were on one of Lynn's trips with our friend Pat Von Ruden and she told me about experience in 2006. They were celebrating a special occasion and decided to rent a Villa that slept ten people. It was located just a few kilometers outside of Siena in the countryside which is quite scenic. Each day they did day tours from their Villa and had a great experience.

I had always kept the website information on the Villa that she had sent me years before. So in early 2016, I contacted Barbara as she was the manager for the family properties around Siena. She only had a two bedroom unit available for one week in September so I booked it. Betty and I discussed it and could not think of two people that we would enjoy the experience with more than Lynn and Bruce. We flew to Florence where Lynn decided she wanted to drive the four of us out to our Villa in Siena. The first evening Bruce and I reviewed the local Tuscany map for our possible destination the next day. It was fun just discussing possible historic towns to visit and tour. We did the same routine each evening. We were planning what old ancient Roman City we would visit the next day. The idea was that we would wander around at a leisure pace through each of them while visiting the historic sites, shops, museums, and churches. Each day we would do a late lunch at a hotel or restaurant where we could experience very scenic panoramic views while eating fabulous Tuscan food and drinking their local wines. For five days we visited five different wine regions and the last day we spent touring Siena.

All in all it was a very special trip. I wandered around those old ancient walled cities like a little kid in awe.

Another trip that was very enjoyable was one to Colorado in early spring, 1982. I was laid off from Farmall in those days because the agriculture industry had slowed down, and tractor sales weren't good. My brothers owned Tri-Star Masonry in Colorado Springs. Their construction business was kind of slow. My brother Mick was always looking for ways to make money. He called me up and said, "Hey, have you ever thought about owning some real estate in Colorado?" I said, "Not really." He said, "Well, I'll make you a heck of a deal. I'll build you an office warehouse building in the south end of Colorado Springs. It will be right off of Academy and Platte, which is Highway 24 that runs through the city on up into the mountains." I said, "Tell me more about it."

It ends up that he designed a three-unit office warehouse building that was about 4,000 square feet. It was to be an all-brick building with a twin-tee flat concrete roof. He thought I could lease it out and collect some pretty good rental income. The proposition made good business sense to me, so I said, "Let's do it."

By that time, we no longer had a mortgage on the house we had built in 1970. So, I went up to the bank and borrowed the down payment as an equity line against the house. Bill McGarry was not very busy in his construction business at that time, so I invited him to ride out to Colorado with me to visit my brothers and investigate the details of Mick's proposition plus what I might arrange for permanent financing on the building. We took the Cadillac on the trip. After meeting with Mick, we went to First Federal Savings and Loan in Colorado Springs, where I arranged financing for the project. The interesting part is that around then, mortgage rates were at 12 percent annualized. Here I am, working at Farmall, making $14 per hour, and I'm constructing this building on all borrowed money. A couple of years later, the interest rate was increased to 15 percent annualized. The good news is that Mick reassured me that, "We can lease it for you and get three tenants in there," which is what he did.

We decided it was a deal and proceeded to have one of his companies build it. Shortly after the construction was completed and the building was leased, we talked about maybe doing another building, which is what we did the following year. And where did I get the money to finance the construction? I used the same two sources as with the first building. One of the things I learned early on in life is that if you don't have much money, you have to figure out a way to leverage what you have. Here we are 35 years later, and Betty and I still own both of those buildings in Colorado Springs. They were paid for years ago, and today we are collecting thousands of dollars of rent each month! Some days it was pretty scary because of the cyclical nature of working in the agricultural manufacturing industry, and I was laid off from Farmall numerous times in the early '80s. Then to top it all off, the local UAW #1309 decided to go on strike for six months because the union did not want to sign the contract that International Harvester offered. Plus, Archie McCardell was the chairman of the board, and he decided he was going to make a statement and break the union! When Farmall closed in 1985, I was paying 15 percent interest on those loans, and I was always a little nervous. I was thinking, "Man, if I lose a tenant, I am going to be in deep doo-doo because I don't have the personal income to cover the payments!"

At any rate, Bill McGarry went to Colorado Springs with me. We had the '80 Cadillac, and were there hanging out. After a couple of days, we pretty much had the business taken care of, so we decided to drive up into the mountains to visit Cripple Creek and Victor, Colorado. Since my brothers were busy, Bill and I drove the Cadillac up the back way to Cripple Creek on Old Gold Camp Road. We drove up behind the Broadmoor Hotel and Resort, which is a hotel John Wayne and all the movie stars stayed at in those days. When we arrived in Cripple Creek (this was before Colorado had legalized casinos and gambling), there was not much activity. We walked around and decided to go into an old saloon. We walked in, and there were maybe half a dozen guys seated at the bar. They were all a bunch of old hippies with long hair, smoking pot and having a few drinks. Bill and I didn't fit in very well in that environment, but we enjoyed observing how the locals were whiling away the day. We also had a good laugh about the scene once we got back out in the street.

Then we went back out of town on Highway 67 over to Victor, which was also an old gold mining town. That town was more like a ghost town, as it was pretty quiet. After wandering around town on foot, we decided to head back to Colorado Springs on Highway 67 and Highway 24.

When we got back to town, we stopped by Tri-Star Masonry's office to see what the boys were up to. They had the bright idea of going out for cocktails that evening since it was our last night in town. Around 3 p.m., we went to a local bar. It ended up being Bill, me, and my three brothers. By the way, all three of them have nicknames. The oldest one, who is the president of Tri-Star Masonry, we called Mickey or Mike, and his nickname is Mort. My second brother, who we all called Dony, is Red Rocks. It has something to do with Red Rocks Amphitheater in Denver. My youngest brother Jimmy is called Doc. I don't know how he got the name Doc, but he'll reveal it to me one of these days.

The five of us were having a good time drinking and laughing. Of course, the next thing you know, we went to another bar. Then later in the evening, we went to another bar. Finally, around 3 a.m., we decided that we had better go to Denny's and have some breakfast, which is what we did. It was pretty hard to believe that I was still driving. And when I drove into the Denny's lot, which had a one-way entrance and a one-way exit, I drove in the exit.

We were making a big scene at Denny's, and luckily they didn't throw us out. But like my youngest brother Doc always says, "I've been thrown out of better places than this!" Nevertheless, we finished our early breakfast and went back over to Mort's house to catch a couple of hour of sleep. We had determined that we were going to leave for home at 7 a.m., and we did. A few hours later, we were driving down the road and started laughing about the fun we had with my brothers the previous evening. We finally settled down and started talking about our experiences growing up, and once I heard Bill's story, I didn't feel so bad about mine. I wasn't the only one who had alcohol issues in my family. He was telling me the story about him and his three siblings. Apparently his dad also really liked to drink. He took off on a binge one day, and he didn't come back for a couple of years. Interestingly enough, one day he finally showed up at the family farm. I believe Bill's mother was a nurse at the local hospital, so they lived a rather modest lifestyle.

It is interesting how you have preconceived images of people you know. Before that conversation, I always thought Bill and his family led a charmed life. That's because Bill bought his wife a new Lincoln Continental Mark III in 1979. It was a gorgeous baby blue car, and it was perfect for Barb, as she was an attractive young lady. She had a wonderful, engaging personality, and when Betty was going through St. Anthony's School of Nursing, Barb was a student nurse at the same facility. Whenever Bill and Barb were out for the evening, they were a striking couple. It appeared that they had really done well, and financially, they had.

By the late1970s, Bill had become quite successful in the home construction business. He and his brother-in-law Charlie Trimble purchased some land and started building new homes on it. They bought 40 acres and built a housing development called Timber Creek. When they had that acreage full of homes, they purchased the adjoining 40 acres and started building houses there.

Then Bill started having back problems and Barb had a lot of allergy issues. At that time, the housing construction business and the economy were slowing down. He and Charlie decided to dissolve the partnership, and Charlie bought Bill out. "You know, with my back issues and Barb's allergy issues, I think we're going to move to Arizona, where the climate will be a much better environment for Barb's allergies."

They pulled up stakes from DeWitt and moved to Fountain Hills, Arizona. Charlie was buying the family farm and farming that while working a full-time job and trying to manage the construction business. He was working day and night. It ended up that Charlie went through a pretty tough financial struggle, while Bill walked off with the money. There was nothing negative about it. It was just the luck of the deal, but that was the end of Bill's luck. When he got to Arizona, his back troubles worsened. He's pretty much bedridden today, which is a tragedy. I believe some of the good health many of us enjoy while others don't is just "the luck of the draw."

Doc, Dony, Billy, Stan, Mick, July 2016

We were driving back home from Colorado Springs that afternoon with hardly any sleep the night before, and it got to be about mid-afternoon. We had been on the road for eight or nine hours when we started giggling and laughing. It was probably one of the most fun trips I ever had in my life. I got to know Bill a lot better, and he really got a kick out of Mort,

Red Rocks, and Doc. He said, "Your brothers are like no three characters I have ever met anywhere in my life!" He said, "Good for them. They work hard, and they have become very successful." And the final comment was, "They sure know how to work, but they really know how to party!" And that pretty much describes how all five of us brothers live our lives.

Stan and Betty Reeg in Athens, Greece, October 2018

Chapter 14

IF THERE WAS NO MONEY, WE'D ALL BE RICH

A Million Is Not Very Much If You Say It Fast

MONEY IS THE ROOT OF ALL WEALTH

One day when I was 11 years old, a thought came to me: Someday I was going to be wealthy. The interesting thing is that as a poor as we were then, I accepted that idea and held on to it throughout my life—and it has proven to be true. Another thought came to me as I was working in the factory in the 1960s and earning $2.70 per hour: I was to be a millionaire by the time I was 40. I didn't reach the goal of becoming a millionaire until I was 54, but I've got to tell you that we've been blessed. Recently, I discovered my first financial statement that was done back in July 1972. It showed I had $28,900 of net worth. Over the years I have always kept track of numbers in many aspects of my life. But most of all, I did financial statements more than once a year for many years. It was interesting to review those older records. The first million dollars is the hardest to make. After the '08 financial collapse, I remember telling my brother Bill, who was a farmer at the time, about how much money I had lost in the markets and in my net worth over the preceding couple of years. His response was, "You should consider yourself lucky. Whoever thought you'd be worth that much money?"

Things then started to improve. In May 2007, A.G. Edwards was bought out by Wachovia Securities, and in November, they paid me a retention bonus check for more than $1 million. So even though I really got beat up in the early 2000s, by November 2007, my net worth was considerable.

The flash of inspiration that came to me back when I was 10 years old has proven to be true. Futhermore, it was all income and net worth that Betty and I accumulated on our own, as I never had an inheritance. Betty inherited $10,000 a couple of years ago when her Mother died, but that is the only inheritance we've ever had.

Quick Hits & Interesting Bits

The first week I was cold calling I was trying to interest potential clients in tax free municipal bond investments. I called Gene Duke, President of H.C. Duke and Co. in East Moline. I figured he was making a good income and paying a lot of income taxes so he might be interested in federal tax free income. My suspicions were correct as he asked if I had any local issues available. It so happened that Dain Bosworth was an originator of local municipal bond issues and fortunately we had some in our inventory.

Once I explained the issue, the interest rate, and the maturity date of the bond he told me he would purchase $5000 worth which is the minimum quantity you could buy. Even though it was a small order it confirmed to me that I could successfully obtain clients and business through cold-calling. It was an exciting experience and gave me the inspiration to call other prospects with the same idea.

◇◇◇

An interesting side note is about twenty years ago, Betty and I became 25 percent owners of the George Wicke estate in St. Donatus. By the time George had died, he was living in only one room of the house! It was a two-story stone house that was built around 1850, and it had a dirt floor in the basement. The roof leaked water so bad that all the ceilings and floors were ruined. When the rain came down, it ran through the roof and second floor ceiling down through the first-floor ceiling and into the basement. The back of the house had a wood-framed kitchen, and the second level was part of a bedroom. By the time George died, the addition had moved four or five inches away from the stone structure.

When we were approached to become investors in the property, the idea was that we would totally gut and restore the house into a duplex. The main floor would be one unit, and the second story would be a second unit, so we would rent them out as apartments and generate some income. Our partners Ron Simon and Rick Putman then tore off the wood addition, and we hired Zeke, a building contractor, to rebuild that portion of the house and build a deck on the backside. Ron and Rick tore off all the shingles and had to replace some of the sheeting on the roof along with all new shingles.

For the second floor, they located the HVAC and heating equipment in the attic. For the first floor, they decided to locate the HVAC and heating equipment in the basement. That meant someone had to dig the dirt floor to a deeper level than it was before we had a concrete floor poured in the basement. Since Rick and Ron were doing all the other work, I volunteered one Saturday to go up and help Rick dig the basement to a deeper level. We had to take it down about 18 inches.

Once we started digging up the dirt, we placed it in five-gallon buckets to carry up and out the back side of the house. It was a tedious task, but we managed to get all the dirt out that day. I am generally immune to physical labor, but I didn't know of anyone else who would be willing to do it that day, so Rick and I did it.

At the same time the construction was going on, a masonry contractor from the country of Luxembourg arranged for a shipment of external surface materials consisting of sand, rose pink-colored paint, and adhesive that was to be applied to the outside stone surface of the house upon completion of all the other construction. When the project was completed, it really looked very nice, and we had people wanting to lease the apartments.

Rick and Ron also replaced much of the stone that had become misaligned on the old barn blacksmith shop behind the house. They installed a new roof, replaced much of the barn board siding, and painted it barn red. It is a nice-looking estate today. We are not making any money on it, but the main idea for me was to maintain another historic structure in the old Village of St. Donatus. The reason I say "another historic structure" is because I received a telephone call from Windy Kalmes in early 1995, and he wanted me to attend a meeting with a group of local people who were reviewing the situation on the Gehlen House and Barn, which is the property adjoining the south side of the Wicke property.

The Gehlen House was built between 1840 and 1850, a few years before the Wicke house was built. You have to remember, Iowa did not become a state until 1846, so this is part of Iowa's early history—when European settlers were coming to the area. In fact, on the Gehlen property stands what we are told by Iowa Barn Foundation authorities is the oldest-standing barn in the state. Construction was completed on the barn in 1839. It is modeled after many of the barns you see in Western Europe. It is what's called a Hausbarn. The farm animals, like hogs, sheep, and cattle, lived on the ground floor, and the people lived on the upper floors. Above the residence was the hayloft. A good percentage of the interior walls are still covered with plaster from the original days when the Hausbarn was built.

Gehlen House in St. Donatus was built in 1840s and added onto later. Now it is a bed and breakfast. It contained the St. Donatus Post Office for many decades.

Gehlen Barn is the oldest barn in Iowa. It's a Hausbarn.

Gehlen Barn, St. Donatus

When Windy Kalmes called, I figured it was some type of "capital call" that revolved around money, as Windy knew I had done well financially over the previous decade. What I soon learned was that the Gehlen property was now owned by a bank in Bellevue, and they were looking for someone to take over ownership of the house, barn, and grounds. Helen Kalmes, her sister Judy Nemmers, and Kim Simon thought the property should be saved and turned into a bed and breakfast and possibly a museum. They were looking to establish an entity and issue stock to the various interested parties. With the proceeds, they would hire a contractor to build out the whole second floor with bedrooms and bathrooms. The main level would have some bedrooms and maybe an apartment or two, plus space for a museum or gift shop. The idea was that Judy and Kim would spearhead the project and manage the operations once it was up and running.

Initially, there were about a dozen different families who invested in the stock to purchase and improve the property. Today, we are down to five parties, as some of the investors wanted out and several of the parties have died. For those of us who are still involved, it has not been a great investment. In fact, we get requests to add capital to the project most years. In the end, it is good for the Village of St. Donatus, so from that perspective, it is a good investment! Fortunately, Rick and Ron do an incredible job of maintaining the facilities and grounds all year or we would be investing a lot more money in the entity.

◇◇◇

Earlier I told you how I was on the board of directors of the German American Heritage Center in downtown Davenport for almost twenty years. I had met Cal Werner back in 1987 or 1988 when I was quite involved in the Rejuvenate Davenport mission in downtown Davenport. At that time I got better acquainted with Ray German of Braren, Mulder, and German.

I believe someday will be recognized for the hundreds of millions of dollars he has raised in the Quad Cities as well as in other parts of the Midwest for some of our great schools and other non-for-profit organizations. He is an excellent fundraiser, and that is a tough job in today's world.

When I say that, what I am referring to is, I believe fundraising in the non-profit and charity organizations in today's world and communities is getting harder and harder to do. At church recently three men were introduced who just finished a huge fundraising campaign. I would say their average age was seventy. And that is probably the average age of most of the fraternal organization members in the United States.

I am not sure how charitable the Gen Xers and the Millennial's are or ever will be? The younger families today are so dedicated to sports activities, dance classes, choral groups, and other competitive events with their children, they don't have time to join organizations nor are they joining fraternal organizations or clubs and many of them I don't attend church any longer. So I'm not sure what the future holds in our country because the values obviously are changing and the priorities have changed with the Gen Xers and the Millennials

◇◇◇

As to Cal Werner, he and I have become the best of friends over the last twenty years. I admire his caring generosity, and much like his father, his humorous spirit. He and I, especially with Ray German's guidance, have raised much of the funds required to build and sustain the German American Heritage facility and its mission in downtown Davenport.

I really respect him so much, as he is so instrumental in the community of Walcott, Iowa, where he is President and a major stockholder of Walcott Trust and Savings Bank and in Davenport, where his father was a prominent attorney for many decades and now Cal as well. He is associated with the

Stanley, Lande, & Hunter law firm as Legal Counsel, and he has made a huge difference in many people's lives through his legal work and all the time, effort, and money he has contributed to the betterment of the whole Quad Cities region.

One of the principles that I aspire to each day is to make a difference, and Cal certainly has been a great example of someone who has done that, and I admire his dedication to the causes he believes in, and I dearly appreciate his friendship and humor!

In 2009 and 2010, the Catholic Diocese of Davenport, after having declared bankruptcy the year before, did a $22 million fund raising campaign and determined that they needed a Board to manage the funds on an unbiased basis. I was invited by Sister Laura Goedken to serve on that Board as the Investment Advisor to the Board. I declined her invitation, but once she came by my office to visit further about the role I could not turn her down. Thank goodness, the Bishop of Davenport Diocese was the Permanent Chair, so I didn't ever serve that role!

For six years or more, I served on the Endowment and Investment Committee with Sr. Goedken and Char Maaske, the Controller of the Diocese. With they and other Board Members we did establish an Investment Policy Statement, along with an allocation model, rebalancing guidelines, performance expectations, a spending policy and a monitoring discipline. After researching many Social Conscious Asset Managers, we decided to hire a Professional Asset Managed firm, by the name of Christian Brothers, in Chicago. Christian Brothers specializes in managing money for Catholic organizations only. They had very competitive institutional level management fees and the performance across the various asset classes we utilized, was excellent.

Once we established all the processes and procedures, I suggested to Sr. Goedken and Char that we add more people with solid financial backgrounds to our committee. I first recommended Rob Arth from Morgan Stanley and then a couple of years later Paul Schnell of Edward Jones. Both of them are true professionals in our Industry and added a lot of valued experience to the process and due diligence for the Committee! I enjoyed the challenge of working with the committee to structure and maintain the best portfolio available for the millions of dollars we were responsible for. I always realized we assumed a lot of responsibility to get competitive returns without taking unreasonable risk, as many donors that contributed to the Campaign worked hard to earn the dollars they donated to the Diocese Future and it is designed to be a perpetual fund! My expectation is the disciplined guidelines we initiated will result in the accounts growing perpetually while the Diocese is withdrawing four to five per cent a year from a growing account value.

◇◇◇

When I attended my 50th high school class reunion a couple of years ago I visited with all my former classmates. I was surprised to learn that one of them, Denny Guenther, was retired and living in Sun City West, Arizona which is across the valley from Scottsdale where Betty and I winter.

The thing I most remember about Denny back in high school was that he was an excellent basketball player. Now that he is retired he plays a lot of golf with his wife Mary and their friends. Denny is Marine Vietnam veteran that was exposed to Agent Orange and as a result has been battling cancer for the last decade.

Our friends Mike and Judy Devine from DeWitt also spend their winters in Phoenix where they have a house and casita. Once a year in March, Mike invites seven of us from Iowa and Wisconsin to join him for a week of golf and cards at their residence. The past couple of years Denny has joined us in that experience.

Baird has a hospitality skybox on the 16th hole of the PGA Waste Management Open in Phoenix. The last couple of years Denny and his wife Mary have joined us for that experience. That famous hole number 16 is the most popular hole on the PGA Tour. It has been a fun experience catching up with Denny on all that has transpired in his life the past 50 years and renewing our friendship.

Stan Reeg and Dennis Guenther enjoy the Waste Management Open from Baird's skybox on Hole 16.

Mary and Dennis Guenther at Waste Management Open,
Phoenix, Arizona, January 2018.

Saturday night hootenanny parties were just an excuse to have
a bonfire at night and drink a lot of beer. I was 14 when we
held them at George Wicke's (we called him Georgie) back-
yard in St. Donatus. Georgie was a bachelor, and he lived in
an old two-story stone house that was built in the 1850s. Out
behind the house, there was a small stone barn that was wood
framed from the second floor on up to the roof. It was originally built as a blacksmith shop. We generally built a bonfire
on the driveway between the barn and house.

Most of the boys my age lived out in the country, and we really
didn't hang around together because there weren't any social
activities. On Saturday evenings, we would get together and
start a nice bonfire. Then Georgie would buy some Trenkle's

wieners, hot dog buns, potato chips, and several 12-packs of Grain Belt beer. Grain Belt pioneered the 12-pack concept. Previous to that, you either bought six-packs or 24-bottle cases of beer. You could buy a 12-pack for $1.70. It was the least expensive beer you could buy, and we generally purchased a good supply so we wouldn't run out if we had a good turnout.

On Saturday evenings, we older brothers always tried to sneak over to St. Donatus, which was only a mile and a half from our house. We enjoyed hanging out and partying with those guys. We had those hootenannies during the summer and fall months for a few years. Back in those days, it's hard to believe, but we kids were drinking alcohol at 12 or 13 years of age! It's amazing we all didn't turn out to be alcoholics, but there was not much for social activity around St. Donatus. Since we were too young to drive, there wasn't anything else for us to do socially, so that is what the older boys around St. Donatus did.

Wicke Barn that Ron Simon and Rick Putman restored.

The former Wicke House, now the 1850 or Kimberly House named after Kim Simon.

Back in the 1970s, there were positive mental attitude rallies and motivational sessions being held around the country in large convention centers and amphitheaters. I remember Betty and I went to Chicago for them a few times. We heard and met speakers like Dr. Robert Schuller, Norman Vincent Peale, and Zig Ziglar.

By this time, we had met a lot of other successful Amway distributors, one of whom was Irv Lynn from Orion, Illinois. I saw an ad in *Success* magazine, which I read all the time, that the legendary William Clement Stone was hosting a one-day PMA (positive mental attitude) workshop at the Hyatt Hotel by the St. Louis Airport. This was 1978, and the cost for the one-day session was $195 per participant.

I convinced Irv, who worked in a skilled trade position at International Harvester in East Moline, to attend this session with me. There were 40 of us in this classroom setting. By that time, William Clement Stone had built one of the most successful insurance companies in America. He also was one of the wealthiest people in America and had written a number of best-selling positive mental attitude and inspirational books. He told his story of rags to riches, as well as many other people's success stories and how their success was attributed to their positive mental attitudes.

The insurance company Stone owned at that time had a unique sales strategy. I won't go into the details because you can Google it, but it was Combined Insurance Company of America. By this time, I was always looking for ways to improve my lot in life, and my goal was to build a successful business and get out of Farmall.

In addition to my Dad's interest in nice cars, I grew up around cars because his younger brothers Eddie, Perly, and Leroy always had nice cars. When Ed came home from serving the Army in Korea, he came by to visit. He was driving a new 1952 black and white two-door hardtop Ford. When Perly came back from his Army tour in Korea, he purchased a 1953 Mercury two-door coupe. It was a dark burgundy—a gorgeous-looking car. In 1956, Perly bought what was the coolest car around Bellevue. It was a two-door hardtop 1956 red and white Mercury Montclair with a red and white interior. That car was stunning and the envy of every young man in the area.

Dwaine Poell became an Amway distributor of ours in the early days, 1973. Bill and Barb McGarry sponsored him and Vicky into the Amway business as part of our organization. At the time, he was distributing the *Grit* magazine to newsstands, grocery stores, drugstores, and display areas in retail stores around eastern Iowa and western Illinois. He was a hard worker and, like myself, always had a sideline business for extra income. He was buying salvaged cars from insurance company pools, restoring them, and then selling them below the average retail price.

In 1970, Dwaine had a beautiful dark blue Pontiac Grand Prix that he had just restored. I saw it in his yard, and it had a "For Sale" sign on it. I stopped by, and it was a stunning car. I thought, "Man, I've got to have that car."

I asked Dwaine, "What do you want for that car?" He told me, "A guy called me, and I promised to sell it to him." I asked if the guy had placed a down payment on it, and Dwaine said no. I said, "What price did you offer it to him at?" He told me he was asking, $3,700. So I replied, "I'll give you $3,800 since you don't have a contract with that guy and he didn't even give you a down payment." He said, "No, I can't do that. I promised him the car at that price, and if he happens to back out or doesn't show up, I'll call you." That is what you call "integrity." I learned that early on from Dwaine.

Dwaine and Vicky became quite successful. He was like me— grew up poor, didn't have any money, and was one of three children. With the integrity that he had and the quality of the work he did, when his cars were finished, they were like brand new. In fact, a few years later, I purchased a 1978 Oldsmobile Toronado from him. He picked it up in Chicago and restored it. It was at the Oldsmobile dealership for service work. It had 620 miles on it, and somebody stole it off the lot. They took the wheels and some other components off the car, plus they damaged the vinyl roof and some of the interior.

It was dark brown with a tan Landau top. It was the last of the large cars—a 1978 Oldsmobile Toronado Brougham. It was a boat, and Betty always hated that car. I bought the car at a good price, then drove it for two years. I placed an ad in the *Clinton Herald*, and a construction worker called me. One Sunday morning after church, Betty and I and the boys drove into Clinton to show the man the Olds. He said, "Man, it's like a brand new car." I asked if he wanted to take it for a drive. He said, "No. It looks beautiful. It's like a new car, and I don't need to drive it." He paid me cash on the spot for it, and I actually made money on it.

By 1969, I was looking for ways to get myself out of the manufacturing world at Farmall. I saw an ad about taking a training course to become an insurance adjuster. A company representative came to our house. He was a hard-selling type person and strong-armed me into signing a contract that day. Basically, he wasn't going to leave until I agreed to monthly payments and making a down payment of $100. It was about a $1,000 commitment, which was a lot of money back in 1969. Then I found out that most insurance companies train their adjusters internally. I called the company, and I was informed that I had signed a contract and there was no breaking the contract.

During that era, Stewart Winstein was a prominent attorney in Rock Island who was on retainer with the UAW Local 1309 Union, which is the union I belonged to while at Farmall. I decided he could get me out of that contract. I paid him $50, and he sent a letter to the insurance adjuster training company. That was the end of them pursuing me, and that was the end of me pursuing a possible career as an insurance adjuster! A good lawyer knows the law. A great lawyer knows the judge!

> "A good lawyer knows the law. A great lawyer knows the judge!"

In 1980, I negotiated a great buy on a Cadillac Coupe de Ville, and we drove that car for nine years. In 1985, when I was living in Minneapolis for my four months of training at Dain Bosworth, Roger Tabor and Mike Gegen were living with me in a fifth-floor riverfront condo. It was in an old warehouse building that had been renovated into condominiums. One morning, I got up and looked out the window at the parking area where I remembered leaving my car the evening before. It wasn't there. When Roger woke up, I said to him, "What did you do with my car last night?" He was a good friend of mine by that time. It would not be unlike him to pull a little prank on me because he knew how proud I was of that car. He said, "Stanley, I wouldn't do anything with your car. I know better!"

We went down to the parking lot and walked all over. It wasn't there. We called the police department. The car had been stolen. They finally found the car on Sunday night in a rundown residential district of South Minneapolis. The thieves had slashed three of the tires. They ripped off the wire-wheel hubcaps. They slashed the dash and took the radio. They slashed the vinyl top. It was a mess. By the time I saw the car, it was in an impoundment yard in Minneapolis, and it looked pretty bad with all the damage they had inflicted on it.

My insurance company said it was not a total loss. They had it repaired, and I drove that car until 1989 when I purchased my first Mercedes-Benz. After deciding to purchase the new Benz, I went to First Central State Bank to talk to Steve Kedley, and I said, "I'm going to sell my Cadillac because I'm buying a new Mercedes-Benz, and I need to borrow a couple thousand bucks." He said, "How much do you want for the Caddie?" and I told him my asking price. By the time I went to the bank the next day to sign the promissory note, he had called a retired friend of his in DeWitt. The next evening when I arrived home from Farmall, Jim Veneable was at my house waiting to see the car. He bought the Cadillac on the spot. It looked like a brand new car and was still in great condition. Jim drove that car around DeWitt for another 10 years, and it always looked good!

Over the past 30 years, I have purchased most of our cars between January and April 1. That is because I did not want to have car payments. Generally, I would be paid my annual bonuses between February and April 15. About six years later, I called Steve again in February when I was purchasing a Cadillac Seville for Betty. I told him I'd be getting my bonus in March, so I needed a 30-day loan to cover the purchase of her Cadillac, which was low mileage and like a brand new car. In Iowa, there are not a lot of people buying cars in February, so it is a good time to get a favorable deal.

He asked me what I was going to do with Betty's current Seville. I told him I was going to sell it. Once I told him the price, he said, "I'll buy it for that." He drove that Cadillac for another 10 years. He took excellent care of it, and every time I saw it, it looked immaculate.

For the last few years before Farmall closed, there was a security guard who was also a disc jockey at KSTT radio station in Davenport. His name was Spike O'Dell, and he was very well liked around the plant.

After Farmall closed, he had high ratings at KSTT, and he ended up at WGN in Chicago, which was a major market and a great move up for him. While the plant closing was tragic for some, a few of us struck it rich because we were forced to go do something else.

My attitude has always been that when one door closes, another door opens—and it's always a better door if you have a positive attitude. I have said that to many people going through career crises, and I am proof of that statement!

I would attribute reading books as the main reason Trevor, our only grandson, is such an excellent student. When his mother Tracy was expecting him, she read to him most every evening. The first time they came to our house after he was born, I had already purchased some books to read to him. As he grew older, I continued to add to his book collection.

After he began walking, whenever they came to our house, the first thing Trevor would do was go in our bedroom and look through the little credenza where we had all of our books, and he would pick out several of them. He and I would sit on the sofa, and I would page through them and read to him.

Going back to when he was a couple of years old, one of his favorites was *The Little Engine That Could.* The story was about a train going up and down hills. The train repeatedly stated, "I think I can. I think I can. I think I can." That story reminds me of when I first started in the investment business at Dain Bosworth. We had some excellent support staff, and one of the ladies was Karen. After I was there a year or so, Karen was diagnosed with cancer and shortly thereafter she gave birth to a baby girl.

Karen said, "I am going to see my daughter graduate from high school." Karen went through all the treatments—chemo and other treatments they gave you back in the late 1980s. Consequently, she lived to see her daughter graduate from high school. When Karen died, her daughter was an adult and a mother. Karen's story shows that if you have a reason to live, you will usually figure out how to survive, no matter what situation you are in!

Many times as a young, inexperienced financial advisor, I didn't know how to get things done. Whenever I had a client ask me how to do something, I would go up front to ask Karen, "How can we do this?" Many times, her response was, "We can't do that!" After hearing this response numerous times, one day I said in an exasperated (and not very nice, businesslike) tone, "Our job is to figure out how we can do things for our clients, not how we can't do things for them! Don't tell me how rocky the sea is—bring the boat in!" Guess what? I never got that response from her again. Once I made that statement to her, she really got on my side. As I became more successful, she was always helpful, proud of what I had accomplished in my career, and grateful she was part of it. In fact, she left Dain Bosworth years later and was a partner in her own financial planning practice.

In my beginning days, there was another person in that Dain office that was very instrumental in my success, and that was Nancy. She was the receptionist who answered the phones at our local office. Since I was making a lot of outgoing calls like the Cold Call Cowboy had suggested, she was always getting return calls for me. If I was on the phone when someone called, she was always very nice to them, with her sweet disposition. She always told them, "I am sure Stan wants to talk to you. If you'll just hang on for another minute or two, I will get him on the line."

Nancy liked the efforts I was putting in to becoming successful. Whenever she received a "Broker of the Day" call, she would try to route it to me. In those days, the "Broker of the Day" was a financial consultant who covered whenever a new potential client would stop in or call our office. Nancy was always very kind and helpful to me.

If you are sincerely working hard to succeed and have a positive attitude, there are always people who will step up to support your efforts. They will do all they can to help you succeed. People in all business relationships want to work with a winner, so they like supporting people who are on their way to success.

◇◇◇

I've played many rounds of golf over the last 30 years but have only scored one hole in one. That happened at Eagle Ridge North Course by Galena, Illinois. It was on hole #4 which is 182 yards and it happened on August 28, 1996, which also happens to be the same day Tiger Woods turned professional.

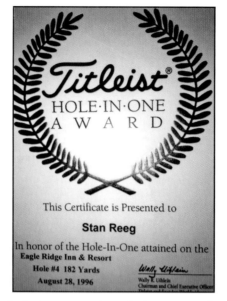

Scored my first hole in one on North Course Eagle Ridge by Galena, Illinois. Same day Tiger Woods turned Pro.

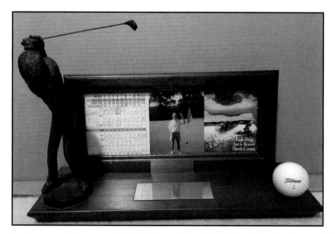

First hole in one, August 28, 1996, at Eagle Ridge by Galena, Illinois.

I was a member of the Davenport Morning Optimist Club in 1987, when Don Decker and Mike Duffy gave a presentation on the many vacated buildings in downtown Davenport and their ideas as to what we could do to improve downtown's visual image. They had created Demolition Davenport and Rejuvenate Davenport as legal entities to get projects done. The next thing you know, I was a board member for Rejuvenate Davenport. Like most nonprofits, we never had enough funds to get things done. From time to time, we would have fund-raising drives where many of us volunteered to visit and solicit contributions from Davenport business owners. Many of the top business leaders in the Quad Cities became involved, either through their executive teams or by personally contributing cash or in-kind services to get projects done.

One of the initial projects we tackled was an old vacated (French & Hecht Wheel Manufacturing) facility that was located on the east edge of downtown Davenport. It was a terrible eyesore. In the midst of tearing down the old factory, a serious coal tar issue was discovered, and this significantly increased the time and cost of the project. Once we got beyond that issue, Lee Enterprises, a huge Davenport media company, built a first-class headquarters building on that site. Among other papers, Lee Enterprises owns the *St. Louis Post-Dispatch* and the local *Quad City Times*. That project gave people the vision that we could significantly improve the image of our historic downtown. From that point on, there were many other projects, and some of them required complicated and complex negotiations with the City as well as owners and developers. The end result is that downtown Davenport looks better today than it has in the last 30 years. As things have progressed, developers from St. Louis and other major cities have come to town and restored some of the old historic buildings and converted them into quality condominium and loft living spaces.

Don Decker and Mike Duffy never received the recognition they deserve for what they did to contribute to the positive economic development activity of downtown Davenport. You do some things in life just because they make sense. You don't need the recognition, but you do know what your role was in achieving the desired outcome.

REINVENTING YOUR BUSINESS

This story took place in February 1994, with clients Duane and JoAnn. They were expecting to receive a significant windfall later in the year, as they were planning to sell their Quad City pay phone business to another entrepreneur. They had phones in 60 locations like laundromats, taverns, other businesses, and on the street corners in phone booths. At the time, they also owned a laundromat. They were a hard-working couple even though he had retired from AT&T after a 31-year career.

We met several times, and they did some retirement plan rollovers and some other investing with me. Then in January 1995, they came in with the proceeds from the sale of their pay phone business. We had already met a couple of times to discuss what they would like to accomplish with the money, and I had laid out an investment plan for them. Initially, they wanted to generate $1,000 a month in additional retirement income with that investment. But, they always were doing something in addition to drawing pension incomes, and they ended up purchasing a tavern that was fairly profitable, so they did not start monthly withdrawals. Today, their account is valued near seven figures and is still growing.

The other part of the story is that when they brought in the check for the sale of the phone business, I asked them who they sold the business to. I figured that person must have some money. They told me his name was E.J. Veit, and they gave me his phone number as well. After they left my office, I called E.J. and had a nice visit with him. He said he owned more than 800 pay phones around the Quad Cities. You must remember that was before the advent of the cell phone technology.

He was looking to possibly own the majority of the pay phones in town and then sell them to one of the major phone companies. But in the end, he kept the pay phone business because it was pretty lucrative, and once cell phones became available, he still had a lot of revenue coming in.

E.J. had a fascinating background, and I always admired the success he made of himself. During WW II, both his parents were killed. So after the War, he and his siblings came to America as immigrants under the auspices of the Catholic Charities Program. The U.S. couple that sponsored them owned farms by Centerville, Iowa, and they viewed the immigrants as cheap labor. They were pretty much treated as slave labor, so once E.J. became an adult, he left home and started selling stainless steel cookware door-to-door.

He was handsome and a good talker, so he had a fair amount of success. Then he got the idea to sell cookware to girls in college dorms and nurse training schools. Then, he added silverware and crystal plus fine china to his line. Since he was used to living on very little money, he continued to build his savings to the point where he started financing all his cookware and china sales and made even more money. By that time, he had become quite successful.

From that business, he moved on to selling home and commercial building security systems. He built that into a very profitable business, then sold it to Mike Duffy at Davenport's Per Mar Security Systems in 1987. Following that sale, E.J. decided to get into the pay phone business. He owned more than 800 pay phones in the Quad Cities area. He liked cars, so he started collecting vintage and unique sports cars and built up quite a nice variety of cars. The pay phone business was declining, so he decided to start a business that his son Cary is still running today. It is called Veit's Vettes & Collector Cars, and it is a thriving, growing family business.

E.J. is a great example of someone who came to American for opportunities and a better life. When he came to America, he couldn't speak English and didn't have any money. Several years ago when he and I were visiting, he told me his net worth was in the millions. He has since passed away, but what he created is still thriving. Many immigrants in the previous generations came to our country for opportunity, and they were willing to work to develop successful lives. They didn't come here for handouts; they came here for the opportunity to become successful. E.J. is a great example of what many other immigrants accomplished in this great country of ours over the past couple of centuries!

What E.J. Veit's story illustrates is this: He built a number of businesses, and as he could see the potential of the businesses declining or leveling off, he would sell them and move on and reinvent himself to do something else. It's a great lesson for all of us, no matter how successful you are. Today, the world around us is changing at a very rapid pace. You had better be changing your thoughts, your processes, and your practices because if you don't, you may be run out of business before you know it. Your business may gradually decline, and it won't ever be the same again.

With the evolution of technology and all of the rapid changes that are going on in our lives, this is one of the most important things to remember. No matter how successful you are, you've got to keep reinventing yourself. You must keep improving systems, have an open mind, and be willing to change what has worked for the last 20 years—because your past business practices may not work so well in the next 20 years!

Just look at small-town America. Small Ma and Pa businesses and family-owned businesses were the lifeblood of the downtown business district of many small towns across America. Many of these got run out of business when Walmart came to town, as Walmart could sell the same product for a lower price than what the average family business owner could purchase it for.

Now the same thing is happening with Amazon in the retail sector of our economy. I would hate to be a retail furniture store, appliance, or clothing store owner today. They are operating in a very competitive landscape. Many people will come in and look at the furniture in your store and then go buy it on the internet and have it shipped direct to their homes. As a business owner, you may have large sums of money invested in brick and mortar plus inventory. Then you are paying insurance, building maintenance, utility bills, and real estate taxes. Your store is also expected to donate to every good cause in your community. That is a tough environment in which to earn a profit! The independent business owner has been the backbone of the U.S. economy in the past century, but that probably is not going to be the case in the next 100 years. You need to change your thinking and change how you are running your business on an ongoing basis.

◇◇◇

After we moved into our new A.G. Edwards office I got to know Rich James, another Financial Consultant in the office. As I got to know him on a personal level, I found that he was interested in purchasing an iconic 1967 427 - 435 horsepower tri-power, four-speed, Corvette, convertible. I realized that he was quite conservative and really hated to spend money frivolously. In those days I was doing a lot of air travel so on most every trip when I was in an airport terminal I would pick up the latest DuPont Registry which featured many exotic cars from across America that were for sale. So, I would highlight any of those Corvettes that were listed and leave the magazine on his desk. Finally, after a couple of years, he succumbed and purchased a 1967 like he desired from a Corvette dealership in Ohio. He wanted to make sure that he was purchasing an authentic original 427 tri-powered car, so he hired a Corvette expert to fly into Ohio from New York to verify the authenticity before he bought it.

It was one of the best things I ever did as a Branch Manager, prodding someone into doing something they wanted to do but almost needed to be pushed into doing. Sometimes we need to give people permission to do something they would like to do. He and his wife Dee had hundreds of hours of enjoyment with that car. Many a spring, summer, and fall evenings he would leave the office early and they would go out for a drive in the countryside with that Corvette. All the times I ever saw him with the car I never saw it with the top up. He loved that car and the joy that they experienced with that car was heartwarming to see!

IT WAS IN THE *DES MOINES REGISTER*, SO HELL, FOR ALL I KNOW, IT COULD BE TRUE

In the early days of my career in the investment business, I subscribed to the daily *Des Moines Register* newspaper because it had an excellent business section, and Jim Lawless was the editor of that section. He featured me and some of the investment equity strategies I was utilizing with my clients in a number of articles. There was also an area in the business section where they featured people who were recently promoted and other executives who were making career changes.

When I read these announcements, I would note if the employees were moving to our area from another part of the United States. The reason is that in addition to changing jobs and residences, they may be changing their advisors as well. Generally when an announcement caught my eye, I would cut it out of the *Des Moines Register* and send it to the incoming person. Then I would try to call the person a few weeks later at the corporate headquarters. The idea was to schedule a meeting with them, perhaps over breakfast or lunch to get acquainted. Whenever I was getting ready to have the initial meeting with the prospective client, I would always get hyped up. Matter of fact, I am still that way today. I realize that each time I meet a new client, it could be a life-changing experience for both parties. And that certainly has proven to be the case with many of them.

Every experience in life is preparing us for our next big step to success whether they are perceived by us to be good or bad, they add to your "gristmill of life." Many young advisors in our business were surrounded most of their lives with affluent people, but that was not the case for me as a Rookie Advisor back in 1985. I was surrounded by good people; they were just not wealthy people. That is why I chose the road of building my business by cold calling initially. In fact, many years after I had become successful, my assistant Tina would challenge me in front of an intern or other rookie advisors to just pull out a random phone number and have me cold call them.

Even though she knew I had built my successful business by cold calling, she was always amazed by my nerve and poise when I would make those calls. Someone would answer or be responsive upon my introduction and the conversation would roll from there. Today, almost all of my good clients are referred to me by their CPA, attorney, another client, or another center of influence. I am grateful for everyone that has referred a prospect or client to me over the years, and I thank them. I believe the reason many of my existing clients don't send me more referrals is they believe I already have all the clients I need or desire. The reality is I can always serve one more client.

My son Todd, along with a few of his friends, started "Cars and Coffee" in Scottsdale in 2007. In the fall of 2017, they were getting hundreds of cars showing up. They moved it to a strip mall area on the southwest corner of North Scottsdale Road and Highway 101, where they can accommodate even more cars. The wonderful thing about that monthly event is that everyone in the Phoenix area brings their cars out for spectators to see. It is the best car show in the desert, and there is no admission fee. Since car collectors of all makes live in the Valley of the Sun, you are likely to see rare and valuable cars you may not even see displayed at national car shows. And, they are all being driven!

Arizona in January—Todd Reeg's "Cars and Coffee"

Disselhorst Family

Shortly after I became the branch manager at A.G. Edwards, my assistant Tina told me there was a gentleman on the phone inquiring if I would be willing to come to Burlington, Iowa, to consult with him and his family. I took the phone call and talked to a man named John. He told me that he and his brother Charles and their father Richard owned Burlington Produce, and they were in the process of selling it and deciding how best to invest the proceeds.

Since they had been working with the local bank, they had already talked to the people in the trust department about possibilities. After a few minutes visiting on the phone, I thought they might be good potential clients for me and agreed to drive down and meet with John and Charles Disselhorst and their father Richard, or Dick, as he was called. On the drive, I wondered if this would be a wild goose chase like some of the experiences I had back in the Amway days when people would answer blind ads and then not show up for the appointment or turn out to be not much of a lead.

When I arrived at their office in the industrial warehouse section of Burlington, it was pretty sparsely furnished, but they did provide me with a seat—a five-gallon bucket turned upside down. By this time, I was more than a little apprehensive. As they told me the story of the successful business they had built and now were in the process of selling, it became apparent they were for real. The owners consisted of Charles and John, who were in their 50s, and their father Dick, who was about 80 years of age. He was a widower, and both of the boys were married.

After they told me their story, I told them mine. I explained how and why I was in the investment business, and we talked conceptually about the type of investment solutions we might utilize based on what their goals for income and maintaining the buying power of the sale proceeds were. They asked me to generate a proposal for them.

We met a few weeks later. Since Burlington Produce was a Class C corporate structure, there was an advantage to owning corporate preferred stocks, as you had to pay federal income taxes only on 30 percent of the income. I noted to them how corporate stock dividends were taxed at a lower rate than bank CDs, U.S. Treasury bonds, and corporate bond income, all of which were treated as ordinary income. I explained the nuances of each of the securities and the advantages of using them in their portfolio. All three of them were shrewd businessmen, so it did not take a lot of explaining on my part. Once I explained my proposal, it made sense to them, and they decided to invest the proceeds—more than $1 million—with me.

By the end of that meeting, I felt like I had built a bridge of understanding and professionalism with both boys and their father. In fact, I believe Dick took a liking to me based on how I respected him and answered the numerous questions he had. Once we establish the relationship, I would call Dick periodically just to stay in touch, even though most of the business was conducted through John and Charles. It ended up developing into a great business relationship and friendship with them and their family over the past 20 years.

This is another example of a little seed that grew into a large tree and is quite enjoyable for all parties involved!

In our business practice, it is very rare to lose a client, except by death. In most of those cases, we are working with their children and grandchildren, so we really don't lose the assets, but we lose the wonderful relationships we shared. The years have passed and sadly so have many of my clients. Except they really weren't clients, they were friends.

No matter what field you are in, there will usually be someone who is more successful than you. Don't be jealous of their success. Instead, use that as motivation that you can even do better. In other words, don't be jealous of other people's success, but be inspired by it. Think, "If they can do it, I can do it." That type of attitude will get you a long way down the path to success in whatever field or career you are in.

◇◇◇

A couple of other gems about becoming successful Tim Skahill shared with me are, "You always fill the other guy's wagon first!" and "Life is not always fair, but if you persist at whatever your goals in life are, you will attain success!" The actions Tim has initiated on my behalf over the last 50 years have helped me immensely. Every time I've talked to Tim, he inspired me to even do better. He also reinforces the qualities he saw in me 50 years ago when I was a young man. If I could just do for someone else what he did for me in my career, I would consider myself a huge success.

I call Tim every six months to visit, and I thank him every time we talk. My wife Betty and Tim Skahill were always very encouraging and made me believe I could become a success in the investment business.

Recently, Tim was telling me about the time a doctor's wife called to inquire about his investment philosophy and experience. The doctor was a prominent cardiologist interested in obtaining Tim's opinion on their investment portfolio. When the topic of fees and commissions came up, the doctor suggested he ought to be entitled to a discount on the commissions. Tim's response was, "If I needed serious heart surgery, I would never consider using a discount heart surgeon."

For many years after that comment, Tim and the doctor enjoyed a successful relationship. The moral of the story is: If you deliver value, people will pay for it. There are no shortcuts to success other than to treat people like you would want to be treated. Always remember the Golden Rule and give people more than they expect. That is the philosophy all five of us Reeg boys have practiced, and it certainly may be a significant reason for our success.

◇◇◇

Once in a while, my wife will say to me, "You'll never grow up," and my response is always the same, "Why would I want to do that?" or "That probably is never going to happen."

For me, there is some magic in living my life in a childlike manner. Have you ever observed the happiness of young children who wander around in awe-inspired wonderment? To them, anything is possible. They can imagine being a teacher, a fireman, a truck driver, a doctor, a nurse, a priest, a minister, maybe even a scientist. If we live our lives more in a childlike state of mind, we could dream up all kinds of possibilities that others never think of. Anybody can grow older. That doesn't take any talent or ability. The idea is to seek out opportunities and change while living with no regrets.

My thinking is "dare to be different." We are only going to make this trip through life one time. Why not go for it in a big way? I believe my brothers have that kind of philosophy as well. We are all willing to step up and take risks. Sometimes it works, and sometimes it doesn't. But, if you don't stick your neck out, you won't get ahead, either. It's like my friend Kathy Mosley told me, "I have not learned much from my successes, but I sure have learned a lot from my mistakes." Wayne Gretzky said, "You miss 100% of the shots you never take."

In everything we Reeg boys do, whether it is work or play, we are all in. In car words, we "have the pedal to the metal." That's why clients like to work with us. They realize we are passionate about what we do and are focused on being the best we can be. My mantra is, "Be in the moment." That means I should not take anything for granted and should be thankful, LISTEN, and be conscious of every aspect of my life.

I realize that as I've gotten older, I have become more learned and receptive to the opportunities that come my way. I have witnessed that other people I meet enjoy being around me. And they want to help me be more successful in all my endeavors. What a great life I have, thanks to all of those cheerleaders!

Success and Goals

I attribute much of my success to my daily morning rituals that I've been doing for the past twenty years. First thing each morning, I read both *Daily Guideposts* and *Thought Conditioners* by Napoleon Hill. My bookmark is a three by three inch card that I have all my goals written on.

Each New Year's Eve before I go out partying, I write down all my goals for the New Year on that card. Every morning, I review them when I am reading the devotionals, and I continue to repeat those goals every morning. It reminds me of what I got up for and what I am working towards each day. You get what you expect and what you inspect. So I believe that habit has been a major contributor to the success I've enjoyed in my life.

I have never forgotten what my Mother preached to us when we were young kids, and that is to start your day with 'morning prayers.' So when I am out on my daily morning walk I tend to pray. Like "This is the day the Lord has made, let us rejoice and be glad in it." Following that I thank God for all the blessings especially the good health Betty and I enjoy. The next is praying for family members, employees, clients, friends, and their families that are sick and or suffering from either physical or mental issues. It is incredible the number of people I know that are dealing with serious health issues and for many it is cancer.

Then, I tend to repeat my self-motivators like, "Day by day in every way, business is getting better and better," "God's power, love, and peace is flowing through me," "I am now attracting health, wealth, and happiness." The other one is "Dear Jesus, please help and guide me to do what is in the best interest of each and every person I come in contact with today." I believe this is a powerful positive way to start the day!

"Stan-isms"

○ You can do it if you think you can.

○ Set big goals and go for them.

○ Get into a career you enjoy and you'll never work another day in your life.

○ Day by day in every way business is getting better and better.

○ Make a plan and work the plan.

○ Mistakes are the stepping stones to success.

○ You either ride life or it rides you.

○ Everything you create or acquire begins in the form of desire.

○ The world stands aside and makes room for the person who knows where they are going.

○ Go the extra mile and opportunity will follow you.

○ The journey of a thousand miles begins with a single step.

○ Success consists of going from failure to failure without loss of enthusiasm.

○ There are those who watch things happen, those who wonder what happened, and those who make things happen.

○ In life, you get in direct proportion to what you give.

○ Determine what you are best at and what you like to do, and develop a burning desire to be the best you can be at it. Then get into ACTION.

To all of you who have read this far, I sincerely thank you for your interest.

APPENDIX

FAST AND CURIOUS

The Reegs Will Talk Cars
at the Drop of a Hat.
Don't Drop Your Hat

FOR GEARHEADS ONLY

When I was quite young, Dad had a 1951 Buick Roadmaster. That was a pretty hot car in the day.

Once he got the Buick up to speed, he would always point at the speedometer and say, "See, we're going 115 miles an hour." At that time, Iowa did not have a speed limit on the main roadways. We Reegs have always had a "need for speed" because we grew up with no speed limit.

When Dad quit drinking in the fall of 1963, he decided, "You know what? I need to buy myself a decent car." He purchased a new Sky Blue 1964 Plymouth Belvedere with push-button drive and a 318-cubic-inch engine. It was a really nice sedan. I would say that was the first nice car Dad ever owned.

Then in the fall of 1965 shortly after I got back from the Army, Dad was talking about buying another Plymouth, a newer one. I said, "You need to buy one of those 1966 Plymouth Satellites." He said, "What are you talking about?" I told him about the car. I said, "You need to get a 383-cubic-inch engine and a four-speed transmission car. Since you like speed, that would be a great car for you." He ordered a new 1966 maroon Satellite. We had a good time with that car, but it was demolished after just a few years when my brothers had a two-car accident on a country road.

In the 1950s, Uncle Perly was working at John Deere Dubuque Tractor Works as a machinist. I was staying at Grandpa and Grandma's house for a few weeks that summer. One Saturday morning, I came downstairs from the bedroom and there on the dining room table were six $20 bills. That was proof he had cashed his check, and he had made more than $120 net on his paycheck after taxes and all deductions for one week. I was blown away by the kind of money he was making at Deere. I had never seen that much cash before as a result of one week's work.

My dad, Bill Reeg, with his 1966 Plymouth Satellite, 383 cu. in. 4-speed.

In the late 1950s and early 1960s, I grew up around relatives who had some pretty cool cars. I've always been around cars. I'm what you would call a "gearhead." My opinion is that there are two types of people in the world: those who buy a car just for transportation and the rest of us gearheads. We love being around cars. We know the details about them. We know all the different models, and we appreciate and are connoisseurs of all the models we own. I have a good Wisconsin friend, Larry Dawley, who is 10 years younger than me. He has owned 23 motorcycles, 87 cars, and five airplanes in his lifetime. He is a true gearhead! I've always had nice cars, at least the best of what I could afford.

Of course, anybody who knows me knows that I am a big-time car guy and have been for many years, going back to my childhood days.

By 1976, I had built up a few resources working at Farmall and Amway. I decided, "You know what? I want to buy one of those '63 Corvettes." Back when I graduated from high school in 1963, that was the new car, and it was a sensational car—very innovative for the day. It was highly desirable and had a rear split window, hence the name, split-window coupe. I decided I was going to go shopping for a Corvette. For many months, I was watching all the newspapers in eastern Iowa, like the *Dubuque Telegraph-Herald*, the *Quad City Times*, and the *Des Moines Register*. I was monitoring the classified ads for 1963 Corvettes.

1963 Daytona Blue Corvette with split windows, photo taken 2003.

One Sunday, we happened to be up at Betty's relatives in Dyersville, Iowa. They had the *Dubuque Telegraph-Herald* there, and I decided to check the classifieds. Sure enough, there was a 1963 Corvette. I said to Betty, "I'd like to call that number and make an inquiry about the details of that car." By this time, I had been on the hunt for a Corvette for months. I was getting impatient. Anybody who knows me very well knows I don't have patience with myself. I have patience with my clients, but not with myself.

Shortly after lunch, I called the phone number in the ad. The owner was the head coach of the Western Dubuque High School football team. When I went over and looked at the car, it was cobbled up. Maybe it had been wrecked years earlier. It had a custom Mako Shark front end on it, which was popular in those days, and it had radiused rear wheel wells on it. The car had five-spoke aluminum wheels with 10-inch wide tires on the back of it. It had side pipes, and someone had installed a pair of gold high-back Mustang seats in the interior, with a fabric that looked somewhat like velour. The exterior was black, with some white pinstripes on the hood, and it had like a 427 Stinger hood. It was a pretty wild car. It wasn't exactly what I was looking for, but it was a '63 Corvette and the price was right, so I bought it.

First Corvette, 1963 split window coupe, Mako Shark modified, purchased Fall, 1977. Note high-back Mustang gold velour seats.

In the late fall or early winter of 1977, I was working at Farmall. Most Fridays at noon, I walked over to the Farmall Credit Union to cash my check. One Friday, I went to cash my check, and there in the parking lot was a Sebring Silver 1963 Corvette Stingray coupe. The paint was worn off on the front fenders, down to the point that you could see bare fiberglass. I just stood there and waited for the guy to come out of the credit union.

A few minutes later, here comes the owner. As he approached the car, I introduced myself and asked, "Is this your '63?" He said, "Yeah, my name's Larry Slenz. I live here in Rock Island, and I work at Farmall."

Larry was not interested in selling the car. He told me what he had rebuilt on it. He had updated the suspension, rebuilt the engine, and installed a new exhaust system. From a mechanical perspective, it was really a nice car. Everything mechanical on the car was rebuilt. I didn't even ask to drive it, as he wasn't interested in selling it at that time. But I did give him a card with my phone number on it, and he gave me a note card with his number on it.

Consequently, every couple of weeks after that, I would go up to his department some time during the day and visit with him about the car. I always told him, "Now, if you ever decide to sell that car, be sure to call me first. Don't bother advertising it; you just need to call me."

I was busy with Farmall, and I was working tons of hours with my Amway business. One Sunday afternoon, I was taking a nap, and Betty woke me. She said, "There's somebody on the phone who wants to talk to you about a car." Sure enough, it was Larry Slenz! He said, "I'm interested in selling the Vette." I said, "How come you decided to sell it?" He said, "I've spotted a '67 Corvette convertible, and I want to buy it."

I paid $5,200 for the car. The next day after work, I picked it up at his house in Rock Island. That car turned out to be a great one! It was somewhat of a project car, but mechanically, it was in great shape. By that time, I had joined the Corvette Club and had met Greg Frew from Sherrard, Illinois. He and his father owned a paint and body shop there. In fact, they were pretty darn good painters because John Deere does all their own painting on all their combines and tractors when they're manufacturing them. But on those pieces of equipment they feature in brochures and at shows, they have those custom painted. Greg and his dad owned the shop that had been designated by Deere to paint all their show machines, and their work was highly regarded.

The car was there for a couple of months. When I got it back, it was painted the original Sebring Silver, and it was stunning! They had taken all the imperfections out of the roof. When the car was originally manufactured, it had little dimples in the top of the roofline, above the doors. When I got that car back, it was straight as an arrow and had a beautiful finish on it. They re-chromed the bumpers, so they looked like new, and we installed new upholstery and carpeting in the interior.

Betty, the boys, and I had a lot of fun with that car because we started taking it to Corvette shows. Within a couple of years, we had earned 18 trophies. As a family, we enjoyed all those experiences together. The only time I ever drove that Corvette was back and forth to shows.

Sebring Silver 1963 Corvette, black interior. Purchased from Larry Slenz in early 1978.

Eric and Stan in 1963 Corvette, Kennedy Mall Show, Dubuque.
We were awarded First in Class and First in People's Choice
Award, 1978.

Shortly after that, I had taken the car by myself on a Saturday
morning to a Corvette show at the Chevrolet dealer in Coralville,
Iowa. There were 40 cars on display inside the dealership, as it
was late winter and the weather can be unpredictable that time
of the year. I was standing by my car, and a well-dressed young
man came up to me and started visiting. He had on a nice pair
of slacks and a sport coat. I'm thinking, "I wonder who this guy
is when he is dressed up like that on a Saturday morning?" He
introduced himself as Larry Winkel, and he was the "Culligan
Man." In other words, he owned the Culligan franchise in the
Iowa City and Cedar Rapids areas. He was quite successful. He
said, "Is this your silver '63?" and I said, "Yes." He responded,
"How would you like to have another one?" I said, "What do you
mean?" He said, "Well, I have a Daytona Blue 1963 split-window
coupe sitting in my garage out at my lake home." I responded,
"If you're going to be around tomorrow, we can set up a time to
take a look at the car."

On Sunday we drove back over to his lake home to view the car. We took it out for a drive, and he told me how much he wanted for that car. I said, "I love this car." Guess what? I bought that car.

First Daytona Blue 1963 Corvette, Winter 1978

1963 Corvette, Daytona Blue, (photo taken 1979)

Unfortunately, I had a two-car garage and I already owned two Corvettes. For one of them, I had rented storage in town at $10 a month. Now I had to find storage for another one, which would cost me another $10 or $15 a month. That sounds like nothing today, but in those days, it was another cost of ownership.

A few months later, I saw an ad for another Corvette. It was a white 1963 split-window coupe in Geneseo, Illinois. It was really a nice car, but not a concours show car. A nice concours car when being judged would score 95 or more points out of a possible 100. It was white with a dark blue interior, and it had a 340-horsepower engine, four-speed transmission, and side pipes. It was a very nice weekend drive car that may have scored 90 points or higher.

1963 split-window coupe (340HP, 4-speed) with Daytona Blue interior.

White 1963 Corvette, 340HP, after new owners mounted knock-off wheels on it. Circa 1980.

I bought that car, so now I had four Corvettes. I stored three of them off-site, and borrowed most of the money to buy them. What I found is, when you have cars that are stored off-site, they are out of mind. Which means you don't drive them or enjoy them near as much as if you have them at your residence. Consequently, that's the reason I have a five-car garage at my house in Iowa. When my son built his house in Scottsdale, he designed two incredible garages. One of them is a four-car show garage, and the other is an eight-car garage with 12-foot ceilings. He can actually install car lifts in the latter and have enough space for 16 cars in that garage.

Being a factory worker, I looked at the Corvettes as a way to have fun, and I hoped to make money on them when I sold them. What happened though is I couldn't afford to pay cash for four Corvettes, so I started borrowing the money. I knew Steve Kedley, who was a loan officer at First Central Bank in DeWitt. I talked to him about what I was up to, and he said, "No problem. You can borrow the money from us. We can just set up notes, and you can pay the interest every six months when it is due." I told him, "I'm buying these for investments, and at some point, I'll be selling them for profit." He had confidence in my ability to pay the loans back, as I had my home mortgage paid off by that time in my life.

At any rate, I was borrowing the money and paying money to store the cars. Once I bought the cars, I was doing everything I could to improve the status of the cars by detailing them and entering them in Corvette shows.

In 1980, I decided I needed to start selling off some of those cars. Those 1963 Corvettes had appreciated significantly by that time. First, I sold the black customized car to a guy from Rock Falls, Illinois.

The next one I sold was the white 340-horsepower car. I advertised it in *Hemmings Motor News*, and I got calls from all over North America. Two brothers from Lincoln, Nebraska, who owned a camera store drove over, looked at the car, and bought it right on the spot. They sent me a picture of it a few weeks later. They had installed a set of knock-off wheels on it, which really made that car stand out.

When I was trying to sell the white '63, an Air Canada pilot called to inquire about it. After our conversation, he flew into Chicago, rented a car, and drove to DeWitt to look at it. That was on a weekday when I was working at Farmall. Betty called me at the shop and said, "This guy is in the garage and when he saw the Daytona Blue '63 in the garage, he decided that he wanted that car instead of the white coupe."

I told Betty to tell him that I didn't want to sell that car. We had bought that car for $6,650 six months previously, and the only thing we did to it was Betty shampooed the upholstery and carpet while I gave it a great wax job. The guy would not leave the house until I put a price on the car. I told her, "If I put a price on the car, he's going to buy it. So, I have to be willing to sell it at that price." I suggested she tell him I would not take anything less than $9,500 for the blue one. As you might imagine, he bought the blue car. He didn't buy the white car that he originally flew in to buy. Later that week, I ended up selling the white Corvette to the brothers from Lincoln who owned the camera store.

Unbeknownst to me, the pilot was planning to drive the blue car to Arizona. He was on vacation and planned to sell it at the Barrett-Jackson Auction in Scottsdale, Arizona, in January. Well, he got to Atlantic, Iowa, which is only about 200 miles from our house. He was driving down Interstate 80 and burned a wheel bearing out on it, so he had to get a wheel bearing replaced. I never heard anything more from him about that car and didn't follow up to see what happened at the auction.

That is the legacy of those three cars. I advertised the Sebring Silver nationally in *Hemmings Motor News,* but I received an inquiry from a guy in Rock Island, just 25 miles away. He and a friend looked at the car and loved it. I showed him all the trophies and awards we had won with the car. I had paid Larry Slenz $5,200 for the car and ended up selling it for $12,000. That one ended up being a pretty good investment as well.

The buyer from Rock Island proceeded to back the car out into the street in front of our house and did a big burnout. That is when I realized he was going to have a lot of fun with that car. From that point on, I decided that no matter how valuable a car is, I am going to drive it, and not just to concours shows. It's like Enzo Ferrari, the founder of Ferrari N.V. of Italy, always said, "Ferraris are meant to be driven." That is true of all cars.

Back to the silver '63. The Rock Island man paid me the $12,000 all in $100 bills. He took the car home and parked it in his garage next to his big boat. He never drove it again and didn't charge the battery. In the winter, the battery froze and exploded. Unfortunately, about two years later, I saw his name in the news when he was arrested for selling drugs.

I made a significant profit on every one of those Corvettes when they sold.

When people get to know me, they always seem to ask, "How did you get into collecting Ferraris?" In January 1998, I called my son Todd, who was working at Bank One in downtown Phoenix. I said, "Hey, I'm thinking about buying another one of those 1963 Corvette split-window coupes." Todd said, "Dad, you need to forget it." I said, "What do you mean?" He said, "Well, with the 'need for speed' that you have, you need to buy a Ferrari." I said, "What are you talking about?" He said, "Well, I took my Mitsubishi 3000GT to a shop to have it detailed. When I dropped the car off at the shop, the owner told me I could take his Ferrari home for the weekend. Well, that Ferrari is a late-model Ferrari Testarossa, and it is the wildest car I have ever driven!" He said, "That is the kind of car you need, Dad!"

We talked about it some more. Todd told me that his future brother-in-law Leo was living in Rochester, Michigan, and Leo's godfather had been a Ferrari collector in the late 1980s. At the time, Leo had a Ferrari 308 model in his sound system business showroom studio.

I called Leo's godfather and visited with him at length about his Ferrari experience. He was fond of the 328 model Ferraris. After a lot of research (this was before the internet), I came to the conclusion that I didn't want to spend more than $100,000 for a Ferrari. So I settled on the idea of possibly buying a 328 Ferrari. Then at Easter, I went to Arizona. Todd and I visited the Ferrari dealer and a number of other exotic sports car dealerships. When I got back home to Iowa, I called both Ferrari dealers in Chicago. They were Lake Forest Motor Sports Cars and Continental Auto Sports Cars in Hinsdale. Neither of the dealers seemed to get any 328 models as trade-ins. That is because the 308 series had a lot of maintenance issues over the years, and I was told that by the time Ferrari had developed the 328 model, they had made more than 1,200 different improvements to those cars. It was a much more reliable vehicle, and owners tended to keep them.

Around July 4, I called Continental. They didn't have any 328s in stock, so I called Lake Forest Motor Sports Cars. The salesman told me, "I have one in the showroom on consignment."

I decided I would drive 200 miles to Chicago and check it out. Since it was a holiday weekend, the only person in the sales department that day was Rick Mancuso, who was the owner. He didn't know me from Adam, and he didn't know if I had two nickels or $20 million, but he spent a lot of time with me that day. The car was a red 1987 328 GTS. It was far from perfect, as it had quite a few chips on the door edges. I could see where the rear exhaust tailpipe had been rubbing up on the screen or the decorative grill that surrounds the tailpipes. I figured whoever had been driving the car had been pounding it pretty hard.

I did not end up buying it, but at least I got to know what a 328 drove and handled like and what the driving experience was like.

The next few weeks, I continued to monitor the inventory of Ferraris at Lake Forest Sports Cars as well as at Continental Motor Sports, and I never saw any 328s. Over the next couple of months, I proceeded to review classified ads in many different newspapers and never really found anything. Then in September, I flew out to Colorado to visit my brothers, as I owned a few commercial buildings out there and wanted to visit the tenants. The second afternoon I was there, I was at my brother's office at Tri-Star Masonry, and I thought, "You know what? I ought to call the Denver Ferrari dealer to see if they have any 328s in stock." When I called the dealership, the salesman responded that he had a 328 GTB in the showroom.

The next morning when we arrived, the Ferrari was parked in front of the dealership in Denver, and it was shining majestically! We talked to the salesman a few of minutes, and then he gave us the keys. We drove it out on I-470 to the west end of Denver in the foothills of the Rocky Mountains. After driving it a few miles, we turned the Ferrari around and drove back to the dealership. As we were cruising along, there was a big four-wheel drive Ford pickup truck right next to my side of the car. Talk about sitting low! When I looked over, my eye level was the bottom of his door, just above the running board. I was thinking, "Man, this car really is a low rider." Later, I learned that from the ground to the peak of the roof is 39 inches, so indeed it is a low rider! That was my first Ferrari purchase.

I was working at A.G. Edwards on Brady Street in Davenport in those days. Horseless Carriage auto movers showed up with my Ferrari around 11 a.m. one day. It created quite a bit of excitement in the neighborhood and our office. Our next door neighbor was a Toyota dealer. I had one of my favorite clients at that time, Bill Meredith, who had been investing with me since back in 1985. In fact, he and his wife were the first clients that ever had more than $1 million invested with me. Bill was a great guy and really enjoyed my company. We made a lot of money for him and Shirley and their family over the years. When I told him about buying the Ferrari, he responded, "When that car shows up, I'm going to be at your office to witness the delivery."

328 GTB being delivered to my AG Edwards office, September, 1998

First Ferrari, September, 1998

The horseless carriage driver had called us a few hours before he was to arrive in Davenport. I called Bill, then I called Betty to tell her to come into town, as we only lived about 20 minutes from the office. It was quite an exciting day and the beginning of a wonderful experience in the Ferrari World!

The car had only 7,800 miles on it. It was a 1989 model, and this was September 1998. So even though it had several owners, it was like a brand new car. Now, 20 years later, I have about 27,000 miles on the 328. In 2005, I was awarded the top points in my class at the Ferrari Club of America National Concours event in Indianapolis. Concours shows generally feature the finest example of a specific model of car. Following that show, I shipped the car to Phoenix, where we entered it into a Concours show in Diablo Stadium, with 120 Ferraris. There, I not only was awarded "Best in Class," but also "Most Outstanding V8 Ferrari." The car has won a lot of awards, and everywhere I take it, people remark about what a beautiful Ferrari it is. I've had a lot of fun with that car and have continued to maintain it at a high level. It may be one of the nicest 1989 328 GTBs in America. That is the story of how I got into Ferraris.

It does not stop there, though. Today, between the cars that Todd and I each own individually plus the ones we own together, we have nine Ferraris.

After the 328 was delivered to my office in Davenport, I joined the Ferrari Club of America, which is how I met Mary and Paul Swartzel from Dubuque. Back in the late 1970s, Betty and I owned four 1963 Split-Window Coupe Corvettes and belonged to the Corvette Club. It was composed of a number of aloof groups, and Betty did not enjoy the experience. Most of the members of the Ferrari Club of America are true Ferrari enthusiasts. They don't care where you are from, how much money you have, how many cars you own, or your social status! That is a totally different experience than I had anticipated and probably much different than what most people would expect.

Anyway, Paul was the regional director for Iowa, Wisconsin, Minnesota, and the two Dakotas. I helped Paul organize events and drives. A few years later, I succeeded him as the regional director. The first organized drive I did with Paul and the Ferrari Club was on a Sunday afternoon drive into Southwest Wisconsin. At our first stop, Paul asked, "What do you think?" I responded, "If we are going to drive this slowly all day, this may be my last drive with the Club." Needless to say, the pace picked up, and Paul and I have done some pretty spirited drives over the last 19 years with our Ferraris!

Being regional director was a great experience because I was able to meet Ferrari owners from all over North America. The vast majority of them are genuinely nice people and a lot of fun.

When I first joined the Ferrari Club, I met some of the people that were involved in the Chicago chapter. We live 165 miles from downtown Chicago. The events they were hosting were published in the *Ferrari Bulletin*, which was a monthly member newsletter. The first time I went to a Ferrari Club event in Chicago, I met Mike Epifanio, who was the regional director.

When I attended Mike's Prancing Horse Roundup for the first time, the event was held on Mike's lawn in Park Ridge. We also used two of his neighbors' lawns to display the cars, as we had about 65 Ferraris in attendance. His next-door neighbor was a Porsche dealer in Chicagoland. When I met some of the owners, I'd say, "Hey, that's really a nice Daytona, or that's really a nice 355," or whatever model of Ferrari they had. They'd say, "Yeah, I've got two or three more Ferraris at home," and I'm thinking, "Why would you have two or three other Ferraris?"

I soon found out. In 2005, Ferrari introduced the new F430 model. I thought, "I would really love to have one of those." One weekend in early 2005, Betty and I were spending the weekend in Oak Brook, Illinois. She loves shopping at Oak Brook, as they have a wonderful variety of retail stores in the outdoor mall. That was a good excuse for me to visit Continental Auto Sports in Hinsdale. I had met Scott Wallace and some of the other sales and service personnel from the dealership at Mike's Prancing Horse Roundup years earlier. And after that initial meeting with Scott, I began to get my 328 serviced at that dealership. It is like many other businesses in the respect that the owner of the business is generally a good clue as to the type of employees in the operations. Many years ago, I met John Weinberger at Road America Track at Elkhart Lake, Wisconsin, as he was a very experienced road racing person. He is a real gentleman, and I can't say enough good things about him and the leadership he has exhibited in his Ferrari and Maserati dealership in Hinsdale.

Continental Auto Sports is quite a nice dealership. From the showrooms, you can see into the service bay area, the lower car storage room, and the wash rack area. I spotted a car that I thought was pretty cool. I found out later that it was a 550 Maranello. That model had almost 500 horsepower, and it was a grand touring car, but I didn't like the color.

When I was talking to my salesman David Alexander, I said, "You know, I really like that car, but I don't like it in that color."

It was around 11:30 a.m. on a Saturday. He said, "Why don't you and Betty go over to the Whole Foods store and have lunch. Take about an hour to do that, and when you come back, I'll have another one here for you to look at."

When Betty and I returned from lunch, there was a black metallic 1999 550 Maranello with a light tan interior and gold brake calipers parked in front of the dealership. The car had my name all over it! I was astounded by the beauty of that car. Betty and I took it for a drive, and when we arrived back at the dealership, I negotiated a deal. I really loved that car and I drove it for two years. At the same time we were at the dealership purchasing the 550 M, they had a new F-430 in the showroom. The practice at that time for most Ferrari dealerships in America was that you would make a $10,000 deposit to get on to the list of potential buyers, and that gave you the right to purchase a new Ferrari at the manufacturer's suggested retail price when your name reached the top of the list. Obviously, I had to have a new F-430, so I made the $10,000 deposit and told Dave that I wanted a six-speed manual gearbox in a coupe model.

1999 Ferrari 550 Maranello, Paradise Valley, Arizona, 2018

1999 Ferrari 550 Maranello, Paradise Valley, Arizona, 2018

I ended up waiting a couple of years. I was thinking, "Am I ever going to get to the top of the list?" Betty and I stopped by the dealership one time when I was going into Chicago to meet with some of my clients. We talked to the sales manager for a bit, and I asked, "Where am I on the list? Am I getting close to the top?" He said, "Yeah, I think you are." He then reached into the drawer where he kept the list of people who were interested in buying the new F-430. As he shuffled through all the potential buyers, he could not find my invoice. A week or so later, I called him. I said, "Did you find the invoice?" He said, "Yeah, yeah, you're getting closer to the top of the list."

A few weeks later, he called me up and he said, "Well, your number is up, and you are going to be able to order a new F-430 coupe." He said, "We need to know all the details and options of what you want on that car." Since I was ordering the car, I decided to tailor it to my desires. Most everyone else was ordering them with the F-1 transmission, which is a paddle shift-type automatic transmission. But me, being a long time gearhead and having always driven sports cars that had four speeds or a stick on the floor, I decided to get a six-speed manual gear box. I ordered a Rosso Corsa coupe, with the ball-polished wheels, which are like a high-gloss aluminum-looking wheel.

I also ordered a leather head liner—the dash and the seats are all hand sewn with an optional red stitching. The power seats and Daytona seat inserts were optional. The seats are black with a one-inch high red Daytona seat accent stripe that runs laterally across the seats. I also ordered it with a yellow-faced tachometer along with some carbon fiber on the dash.

2007 F-430 in my garage, 6-speed manual transmission.

The car was delivered to Continental from Italy in July. I asked my good friend Steve Wolfe if he would ride into Chicago with me on Saturday July 27 to pick up my new Ferrari. He brought along a digital camera to photograph me taking delivery of it. He took pictures of me writing the check for about $200,000 for the car, as I paid cash for it. When we were ready to leave the dealership, the car was parked right out in front of Continental Auto Sports' shop, which was a pretty cool building. He took a picture of me in the car as we were getting ready to leave. Once we got out on the highway, he was driving my Mercedes-Benz back home, and he took all kinds of pictures of the Ferrari. What a great guy he is! Three weeks later, he came out to the house and gave me a DVD with all those pictures on it, plus a 20 by 30-inch framed photo of the F-430 in front of the dealership on the day of delivery. I will always have that as a keepsake.

Over the years, Steve has become one of my best friends. This is because he cares, he pays attention, and he does special things for people. That's why he's a friend to a lot of people. Over the years, he, his wife Karen, Betty, and I have had a lot of fun doing Sunday drives out through eastern Iowa, into southwestern Wisconsin, and over around Galena on some of those scenic two-lane roads.

Several years before that, I had talked to Dr. Jack Frost in St. Donatus about possibly buying one of his Ferraris. I had been hounding him for about three years to sell me one of his Daytonas. At one time, he owned three of them! Finally, one Tuesday afternoon, his son Greg called me at my office and said, "Hey, Dad's going sell the 1972 Red Daytona coupe, and you always told him you wanted first chance on it. When do you want to come up and see him?" I said, "Well, I can't come up until Saturday morning, but I tell you what you do—make sure you have all the books and records for that car. I would be interested in any extra wheels or other parts that your dad has and, most of all, make sure that you have the title there. I'll bring along a check." We talked about Doc's asking price, which was about $50,000 more than it had been three years before when I started chasing the car. Nevertheless, it was a one owner, unique car and a good buy. My brother Bill, who was a nearby farmer, went with me to pick up the car.

Dr. Jack Frost with three very low mileage Daytona Ferraris on his St. Donatus driveway.

When we arrived, we did all the paperwork and took a number of pictures. Since the car did not run and didn't have any brakes, we had to tow it out of Doc's property. We hooked up a little tractor behind the car with a rope. In front of the vehicle, we placed a little four-wheeler that a lot of farmers use for herding cattle, and we tied a rope to the front of the Daytona.

Instead of riding horses like farmers and ranchers did years ago, they now use these four-wheelers. In rural areas, there are a lot of people who own recreational four-wheeler vehicles these days. When you drive throughout eastern Iowa, south-western Wisconsin, and northwestern Illinois, you'll see them parked in many farmyards.

We hooked each of those vehicles up to the Daytona and towed the car down to St. Donatus Body and Paint, which is only about three blocks away from Doc Frost's house. St. Donatus Body and Paint is owned by Greg and Jeanie Kalmes. Greg has been in the auto repair and restoration business for the last 40 years, and Doc had him do all his paint and body work repairs during those years. Greg is an amazing person, as he treats every project as if it was his own. Not only does he do a great job on the fit and finish on the cars he restores, but he has done a number of paint jobs on cars that have been awarded "Best Paint" at national car shows.

June 24, 2006, the day I purchased the Ferrari Daytona from Doc Frost asking Doc, "Who would have ever thought one of those 'Reeg Boys' would ever buy one of your Ferraris?"

Engine didn't run and had no brakes so my brother Bill and Greg Frost are towing it down to Greg Kalmes' St. Donatus Body & Paint and I just wrote Doc a $125K check for it!

I came home later that afternoon, and Betty said, "Where is the car?" I said, "Well, it doesn't run and it doesn't have any brakes." She said, "And you paid $125,000 for a car that doesn't run?" She was astounded and a little bit miffed. Betty appreciates a nice car, but to her it's just transportation. Although I've got to admit, she enjoys the social events we attend and the friends we have made through the Ferrari Club of America over the last 20 years.

My friend Paul Swartzel has been a long-time Ferrari owner. So, I had Paul, Greg Kalmes, and Ron (who works at Greg's shop) coordinate getting the car running—replacing all the brake components and rebuilding everything from the brake lines and hoses to the master cylinder and all the calipers. We renovated and updated the whole braking system on the car. Then Ron and Paul went to work on getting the engine running. They drained the fuel tank to make sure there wasn't any contaminated fuel in the tank.

It was several weeks later when we got the car running. One Saturday morning, I drove up to meet Paul at St. Donatus Body and Paint, which is exactly 50 miles from my house. That is where we stored the car. By then, Paul had a new exhaust system installed on the car because the exhaust pipes were all rotted and rusted. Paul and I drove it a few miles that day. We weren't sure if the gas gauge worked, and after driving it about 40 miles, of course, we ran out of gas. Fortunately, we were close to Dubuque, but it still was a little embarrassing. Here we are sitting alongside Highway 61, which is a four-lane highway, with no gas or gas can. We walked a few blocks to a small gas station in Key West. Fortunately, they had a gas can for sale, and we were able to fill it up and walk back to the car. We poured the contents into the tank, and the engine started up right away. We drove straight to a gas station and put more gas in the tank.

We were only a few minutes from Paul's house, so we thought we would drive over and show his wife Mary the car. By the time we arrived at his house and parked on the driveway, there was all kinds of smoke coming out from under the Daytona. I was quite concerned. After looking under the hood and underneath the car, we realized the new stainless steel exhaust system had been painted black, and the paint was burning off the pipes. Wow, was I relieved!

After showing Mary the car, we drove it back down to St. Donatus, as I had decided I would leave the car with Paul to tinker with and drive the following week to get some of the kinks out and make sure everything was functioning properly. The following Thursday evening, I received a call from Paul. Paul and Mary were driving at speed over by Galena Winery, and all at once, there was smoke and oil spewing out from underneath the hood onto the windshield. This time, it was more serious. Paul turned the ignition off right away and coasted to the shoulder of Highway 20. Thank God, I wasn't driving it, as I would have probably had the engine revved up and created more damage than he did!

He proceeded to tell me, "Hey, there's something seriously wrong with that engine."

Paul had the car towed to Greg's shop, and we agreed to meet again on Saturday morning to determine what had happened. Greg, Paul, and I considered the possibilities and who we would have work on the engine. Greg highly recommended Bob Siegwarth from over by Otter Creek. The reason he recommended Bob is that he specialized in rebuilding high-performance engines for guys that did drag racing and stock car racing, and he had a dynamometer in his shop. We called Bob, and Greg hauled the car over to his shop, which was 15 miles away.

Once Bob tore the engine down, he saw that we had turned a bearing on the crankshaft. So we ended up having to do a total engine rebuild. We were fortunate in that they were able to balance and polish the crankshaft at a specialized shop in Rockford, Illinois. We were lucky because I don't know where we would have been able to obtain a replacement crankshaft, as these are rare cars and anything like that would not only be hard to find, but would probably cost more than $25,000. Over a period of five years from 1968 through 1973, Ferrari manufactured only 1,260 of these cars. Paul quarterbacked the engine rebuild with Bob and obtained all the parts needed to rebuild it. This is not like rebuilding a Chevy or Ford engine for a couple thousand dollars.

By the time the engine rebuild was complete, the cost was $28,000. I could have bought a pretty nice car for that money, but this is a historic Ferrari! Keep in mind, Doc Frost had taken delivery of this car in Modena, Italy, in March of 1973, and the speedometer had only 16,091 miles on it when I purchased it from him. Most of those miles were registered on the car when he had shipped it to Europe and did extensive touring with it there. In fact, in the back window of the Daytona, he had placed decals of the various countries he and Luella toured with the car, and they are still there today.

Once Bob completed the engine rebuild, he placed it on his engine stand and hooked it up to his dynamometer. He ran it on the dyno for about 11 hours and did some calibrations and settings on the engine. He verified the 352 horsepower that it originally came with from the factory. I have all the calibrations and printouts of the tests he did on the engine, and they are recorded in a three-ring binder that contains the history of the car. Bob also photographed the whole disassembly and reassembly process as he did the rebuild to verify what he had done.

The engine ran very well after that. The car had 30-year-old tires on it when I took delivery from Doc. So, we ordered new Pirelli tires, and I replaced all four of them. When I purchased the car from Doc, he provided me with several sets of wheels. In fact, the one set is the four Chromador aluminum wheels with the original Michelin XWX tires on them, from when he took delivery of the car in Italy back in 1973. I also have two sets of Borrani wire wheels for it.

One fall Saturday morning in November, my son Eric was visiting us from Des Moines, and I asked him if he would like to go for a ride in the Daytona. Of course, he did. So we drove it around DeWitt a bit to get the engine and oil temperature warmed up, and then I headed west of town on a rural asphalt two-lane road, where I cranked it up to 150 miles per hour. In the last 12 years since I've owned the car, that is the only time I have driven it that fast. It is a fun car to drive and is an amazing experience to drive at high speeds, especially when you consider it is of that vintage. When it was manufactured new at the factory in 1973, the Daytona was considered the fastest production car in the world.

The car had pretty much just sat in Doc's heated and air conditioned storage building for the past 25 years. It was one of those cars that looked good when you were 15 feet or further away, but when you got up close, it had cracks all over the body that made it look like a spider web. The paint had cracked all over the body. As I started driving it more, the paint just started peeling and flying off the body when I was driving down the road.

I knew at some point I was going to have to strip the paint down to bare metal and repaint it. But, I had decided I was going to drive the car for a while to make sure all of the mechanicals were in A-1 condition before painting it. I didn't want a mechanic leaning over the fenders on a brand new paint job! I drove it that way from late 2006 until January 2008, when I took it back up to St. Donatus Body and Paint. Greg and I had been discussing what to do. In the end, we decided to do a total restoration on the car. He did not remove the suspension from the car. In other words, he did not do a frame-up restoration, but he cleaned it and painted all the suspension components the original factory colors. When he had the engine out, he painted the cowl, underneath the hood, the fender wells, and all the other components that were to be black. We kept the original interior and carpeting and reinstalled them when the paint work was completed. The interior really needed a lot of attention and detailing. When Greg was finished with the restoration, it was spectacular!

When Greg works on your car, I don't care if it's a Mustang or if it's a Ferrari, he treats it as if it were his own. He is detail oriented. He removed all the glass from the car and stripped the paint down to the original metal surface. He did some welding around some of the door edges, as some of the gaps around the doors, hood, and fenders were not necessarily uniform when the car was manufactured at the factory. Greg, being a perfectionist, made sure the fit, finish, and lines were perfect. He had a lot of pride when working on that car because all the years Doc owned the car, Greg did all the body and paint work on it. And now he was getting the opportunity to make it look even better than when it was new.

Finally, Greg repainted it. The car was in his shop for a little over one year. I got it back in the spring of 2009. We still had a lot of cleaning and detailing work to do on it. The Ferrari Club of America was hosting an annual meet and Concours show at Elkhart Lake, Wisconsin, at the Road America track in July 2009, so I decided to register the car for the National Ferrari Concours Show.

We borrowed Doc Frost's car hauler from his son Greg, and my brother Bill and I hauled the car to Elkhart Lake. When we unloaded the car from the trailer, the finish on the Daytona looked like it was wet. The paint finish was spectacular, and it looked perfect. Interestingly enough, we did the Concours show on the grounds of the Osthoff Hotel right there on the lakefront of Elkhart Lake. After all the results were in, my Daytona was awarded the highest points in my class. There were several other nice Daytonas and 330 GTCs in my class, but I walked off with top honors in the class. I was pretty excited about that. Thirty-three years previous to that, Dr. Jack Frost had displayed the Daytona at a National Ferrari Club of America Concours in Grosse Point, Michigan, on the lakefront, and it was awarded the top points in its class. I actually have a photo of the magazine verifying the award in 1973.

Since that time, I've had it to Savannah, Georgia, for the Ferrari national meet. I've taken it out to Pebble Beach for the national Ferrari show. I've had it to Palm Springs, California, for an FCA national meet. I've taken it to a number of other national events around the country, and each time, the car has been highly recognized.

1973 Prancing Horse

In 2015, when the second annual Concours d'Elegance of Arizona was being held at the Biltmore Hotel in Phoenix, my Daytona was invited to participate. The Arizona Concours d'Elegance was held each year in January. There were 85 cars invited to that show. There were five different Ferraris, but mine was in the classic car class, competing with other vintage European cars like Porsche, Jaguar, and Mercedes-Benz. The Daytona was awarded the class award at that show, and I'm pretty proud because the class was not just Ferraris. It contained some cars that had total frame-up restorations, and they looked better than when they came out of the factory new.

The second award the Daytona received was the "Best Story Car" of the Concours event. The reason is because it was a 1972 Ferrari that Dr. Jack Frost had ordered in September 1972 from Bill Harrah's Modern Classic Motors dealership in Reno,

Nevada. Yes, that is the same Bill Harrah who owned Harrah's Casinos.

Doc's Daytona was one of 85 cars invited to the Second Annual Arizona Concours de Elegance, January 10, 2015. Won Class Award and "Best Story of Car" Award.

Decals of European countries car was driven in.

Doc ordered the car in September 1972, and it was ready for delivery by March 1973. He and Luella and their 16-year-old son Mark flew to Italy and hired a driver to take them out to Modena to pick up the Daytona. I have a photo of Mark kneeling beside the Daytona in the factory lot alongside other new Daytonas and Dinos. They then travelled several different countries in Europe with the Daytona, as they were there for three weeks when they took delivery of it.

Doc always documented his travels to and around Europe, especially when he was on buying trips. He documented all the family's activities during that visit, and he including many details, accounting for every penny he spent each day. I have numerous pictures of the Daytona at historic sites in Europe. One of them happens to be at Normandy Beach with the car parked on the waterfront. In the background, you can see a WWII sunken ship. In fact, I have the envelope and itinerary that their Ozark Airline tickets from Dubuque to Chicago were delivered in. I also have the international flight schedule as well, which I believe was with TWA.

In 1981, Doc and Luella were going back to Europe for an International Dermatology Convention and Workshop, so he decided they would take the Daytona and travel for a few weeks while they were there. He arranged a first-class state room on the QE-2 for themselves, and the Ferrari was stored in the cargo area below them. Those five weeks, he documented every day's activities, the 5,729 miles they drove the Daytona, and how much money they spent. Consequently, the reason I received the "Best Story Award" is because I had all the documentation to prove the history, while other owners had just stories about their cars.

I am fortunate to have known Dr. Jack Frost and his family for many years and to be the second owner of the Daytona. I've had a lot of fun with that car. In fact, on February 10, 2018, we displayed it at the Concours in the Hills that was held in Fountain Hills, Arizona. It was recognized as the "Best Pre-1973

Ferrari" at the show. They had about 700 cars in attendance, so that was a nice honor.

It all goes back to June 25, 2006, when I purchased the car from Doc Frost. I told him SN 16213 would always be known as Dr. Jack Frost's Daytona. I have met people at Ferrari events around the country where when they see the car with all the books and records, they remark, "I knew Jack Frost!" He would be proud that his legacy lives on, even though he died six months to the day after he sold me the Daytona. I view this exotic car experience as us just being caretakers for the next generation of owners.

Speaking of the Arizona Concours d'Elegance show, the first one was staged in January 2014, and there were 80 cars invited to the event. My son Todd and his 330 GTC were invited. There were only five Ferraris invited. His 330 was in the preservation class because it is an all original car. It has the original paint, original interior, and original engine, and Todd has spent hundreds of hours detailing and cleaning that car to the point where it is immaculate. It looks much better than it did when he purchased it from the previous owners. They were the second owners and had the car for more than 30 years. The previous owner was a retired Navy officer and, much like Doc Frost, he had taken great care of the car and documented everything he ever did to it. The car was sold new in Arizona, and it always had been in the dry temperate climate of Arizona. It was in excellent shape. It just needed some tender loving care. At the Arizona show, Todd's 330 GTC was awarded the "Best Preservation Car" in the field. I will never forget how excited Todd and Jodi were when they drove the car past the award stand that Sunday!

First Arizona Concours Top Preservation Award to Todd and Jodi in their 1967 330 GTC, January 2014.

We view these cars as portfolio diversification in our investment portfolios. We try to purchase special Italian cars that are in nice condition, and we take them to where they become national show winning cars. We are fortune in that we have Steve Mroviak as a personal friend here in Arizona, as we on our own would not be able to do the technical quality and perfectionist-type work that he does. He is very skilled and recognized as an expert on the national level. In fact, he is currently a judge at some of the national exotic European car shows.

Every exotic car Todd and I own has a story behind it, but it may be boring for you to read through all the details. It is not an ego trip for us. It is something we love to do together. Most of the cars are older, desirable Italian cars and will continue to appreciate in value over time. Therefore, in addition to us driving and showing them, they may turn out to be great investments as well.

In January of 2002, one of my friends and clients was Kevin Jensen, and he had a 1967 Corvette, a 435-horsepower, four-speed, black car with a red stinger hood and a black convertible soft top. The car had red leather interior, which was pretty rare because most of them had Naugahyde.

He was storing the car at Todd Spain's building in Elwood, Iowa. Todd had done some work on Kevin's car, and it was being stored in his warehouse, which was formerly the school gymnasium. Todd Spain's business is called Twin Oak Collector Cars. Todd had purchased the Elwood Community School, which had a gymnasium and classrooms attached to it. He used the classrooms for Corvettes being staged for restoration. Once the restoration was completed, he would store them in the gymnasium, where the whole floor was covered with 4 by 8-foot sheets of particle board.

We went in the gym to view Kevin's car. It was a beautiful Corvette. After I had looked at it for a while, I walked around the gymnasium to look at the other Corvettes. At the end of the aisle was a 1963 Corvette split-window coupe. It was my favorite color, which is Daytona Blue, with a dark blue interior, and it was a 300-horsepower car with a four-speed transmission and knock-off wheels on it. Most buyers ordered their 1963 Corvettes with hubcaps because one of the most expensive options, other than fuel injection, was the knock-off wheels.

1963 Corvette Daytona Blue with knockoff wheels, 2004

1963 Corvette, photo taken at Todd Spain's Twin-Oaks Corvettes in Elwood, Iowa, 2002

The car looked really nice, and I said to Todd Spain, "What are you doing with this car?" He said, "I have it here because I am just doing a little detail work for the owner." He said, "The gentleman is from Ohio, and he is going to sell that car, so he wants me to advertise it in *Hemmings Motor News*." I said, "How much is he looking to sell that car for?" He said, "Well, $33,800."

I critically reviewed the car to be certain that the body lines were all good on it. The paint was good, and the interior was in excellent condition. I said, "You know, I'm quite interested in this car." I bought that car in early 2002 for $33,800, and I drove it for 2 ½ years. In January 2005, the price of these 1963 Corvette coupes had risen significantly. I had a good friend that found a buyer for me, and I sold it for $68,000.

1972 Ferrari Daytona, Fountain Hills, Arizona, February, 2018

REEG FAMILY HISTORY

Bill and Marian Reeg, August 1, 1945

Johann Adam Reeg was born in Kirch-Brombach, Germany on 11-5-1771. He married Anna Christina Friedrich from Kirch-Brombach on 9-1-1795. Their son George Adam Reeg, also known as Johann Adam Reeg, was born on 11-5-1802 in Kirch-Brombach. Johann married Elizabetha Haas on 1-27-1824 in Vielbrunn, Germany. They were married in the German Evangelical Lutheran Church which was built in 1494. The Reeg's have lived on the Haas family estate since that time. The Estate in Vielbrunn consists of a hausbarn which was built in the 1400's and other farm buildings that are surrounded by 125 acres of farm ground.

Vielbrunn, Germany
Reeg Estate circa 1930s, this house is over 500 years old.

Their fifth child Johann Konrad was born on 2-4-1831 and at twenty years of age immigrated to America in 1851. He initially settled in Lancaster County, Pennsylvania, and married Elizabeth Sheler in 1852. They then moved to Bellevue, Iowa, in 1855 and he was known as Conrad Reeg.

It is recorded in the Jackson County Historical records of 1876 that Conrad owned 320 acres in Sections 17 and 18 of Bellevue Township, four miles west of Bellevue in Paradise Valley by the Big Mill Creek. Conrad was one of the founders of the German Evangelical Lutheran of Bellevue and was a member of the German Evangelical Lutheran Synod of Iowa. The Church was founded in 1868 and Conrad was an initial officer. It was a 30 by 50 foot concrete structure that cost about $3300 to build. Today it is known as St. John's Lutheran Church and is an extension of the original building. It was noted in the 1890 Jackson County Historical records that Conrad and his family were Lutherans and Republicans.

He and Elizabeth Sheler had seven children of which the third was Adam Reeg who was born 8-16-1859 in Bellevue. Adam married Sophia Siemers on 10-16-1883 in Bellevue, Iowa. They had four daughters and one son born 2-7-1892 named William John Reeg. William J. Reeg and Edna Ernst were married on 8-2-1922 and their first born of eight children was my dad, William Adam Reeg.

It appears all the Reeg ancestor's from my Grandpa through the previous generations in Germany back to the 1700's were all farmers.

This was based on all the historical records I have obtained on the Reeg Family history over the years.

Stanley M. Reeg of DeWitt, Iowa
October 30, 2018

The original Reeg Coat of Arms was bestowed on Wolf Christoph Reeg in 1574 at Nuremberg, Germany.

ACKNOWLEDGMENTS

For the past five or six years, my oldest son, Todd, has been encouraging me to write the story of my life. Generally, most children end up becoming better educated and more successful than we are as their parents, and that is his case. Nevertheless, his comment was, "You are the epitome of the great American Dream! You grew up poor and have become a multimillionaire by taking advantage of the opportunities that came your way." "And, I would like to see you document your story for the benefit of future generations of our family."

Then last year Rich Wolfe comes along and he says to me "Are you really from St. Donatus?" I told him "yes". He tells me "You are different that anyone I've ever met from St. Donatus, you have a heck of a story, and I'd like to do a book on you."

The reason you might want to read this book is: if you have a dream of being exceptionally successful in life, I may share a couple of ideas that may give you the inspiration that you, too, can make your dreams come true in this great country of ours! What I have found in life is if you want to be successful, talk to the top people in your field, as they are always willing to share their ideas and thoughts with you.

I have many people to thank for the success I have achieved, and the first would be my wife of 50 years, Betty McCarthy Reeg. Both of my parents, Bill and Marian Reeg, who passed on many positive attributes which were lessons that I've never forgotten. Also my siblings, many friends, and wonderful business leaders and clients that have inspired me to be the best I can be in whatever endeavor I am pursuing. I would like to thank Windy and Helen Kalmes for their inspiration. Kelly Auliff, Tina, Stephanie Witt, Heather Rushenberg, Tracy Thumann, and all those who have helped me serve my clients over the last 30 years. Rich Wolfe my co-author and publisher as well as Wendy Ledger, Dale Ratermann, Michael Ricigliano, Andy Hansen, and Lisa Liddy whom without their assistance and guidance this book would not have been possible.

I am wishing you all the success you can dream for and hope you enjoy this story!

All the profits from the sale of this book are being donated to the Paul B. Sharar Foundation of Clinton Community College, where thirty-three years ago, I participated in a week-long Career and Assessment Evaluation class. That was the beginning of my inspiration to becoming an Investment Advisor.

If you would like to order more copies of this book, please go to Amazon.com.

Other Books by Rich Wolfe

For Bronco Fans Only
For Browns Fans Only
For Buckeye Fans Only
For Cardinals Fans Only—Volume I
For Cardinals Fans Only—Volume 2
For Clemson Fans Only
For Cubs Fans Only
For Cubs Fans Only—Volume II
For Georgia Fans Only
For Hawkeye Fans Only
For Kansas City Chiefs Fans Only
For K-State Fans Only
For KU Fans Only (Kansas)
For Mets Fans Only

For Michigan Fans Only
For Milwaukee Braves Fans Only
For Mizzou Fans Only
For Nebraska Fans Only
For Notre Dame Fans Only—The New Saturday Bible
For Oklahoma Fans Only
For Packers Fans Only
For Phillies Fans Only
For Red Sox Fans Only
For South Carolina Fans Only
For Yankee Fans Only
For Yankee Fans Only—Volume II

And the Last Shall Be First (Kurt Warner)
Been There, Shoulda Done That (John Daly)
Da Coach (Mike Ditka)
Fandemonium
He Graduated Life with Honors and No Regrets (Pat Tillman)
I Love It, I Love It, I Love It (with Jim Zabel, Iowa announcer)
I Remember Harry Caray
I Saw It On the Radio (Vin Scully)
Jack Clifford (The Food Network Founder)
Jeremy Lin, The Asian Sensation
Jim Harbaugh—Coach
Joe Maddon—Hallelujah, We're Gonna Party Like It's 1908
Knightmares (Bobby Knight)
Oh, What a Knight (Bobby Knight)
On The Road—A Season With College GameDay (Coming Soon)
Personal Foul (With Tim Donaghy, former NBA referee)
Remembering Dale Earnhardt
Remembering Harry Kalas
Remembering Jack Buck
Ron Santo, A Perfect 10
Sports Fans Who Made Headlines
Take This Job and Love It (Jon Gruden)
The Real McCoy (Al McCoy, Phoenix Suns announcer)
There's No Expiration Date on Dreams (Tom Brady)
Tim Russert, We Heartily Knew Ye
Tony Gwynn...He Left His Heart in San Diego

Free Super Bowl Tickets- Rich Wolfe author stories

All books are the same size, format and price.
Questions or to order? Contact the author directly at 602-738-5889.